Across State Lines and Elections

A Political and Historical
Aspect of our State Elections

Paperback ISBN: 979-8-218-55900-7

Printed in the United States of America

16 17 18 19 20 21 XXX 9 8 7 6 5 4 3 2 1

CONTENTS

Article I, Section IV, Clause I

"The Times, Places and Manner of holding Elections for Senators and Representatives, shall be prescribed in each State by the Legislature thereof; but the Congress may at any time by Law make or alter such Regulations, except as to the Places of chusing [sic] Senators.

Article II, Section I, Clause II

"Each State shall appoint, in such Manner as the Legislature thereof may direct, a Number of Electors, equal to the whole Number of Senators and Representatives to which the State may be entitled in the Congress: but no Senator or Representative, or Person holding an Office of Trust or Profit under the United States, shall be appointed an Elector.

PREFACE

The electoral structure of this nation, the United States of America is quite different and stands out from other countries' own electoral codes and structures. This nation was established to be in different with other nations. This union of indivisible sovereign states were to be independent from one another and independent from a central authority. The first order of independence was supposed to be within their election of officers to their state legislatures, their representation to the national Congress, and presidential elections. The election enforcement belongs in the hands of each state and its citizens.

Each state is different from one another and hence why the constitutional framers made it known to create their new nation this way. The Constitution is indeed a living document but must remain living in its original intent. The document can be changed but the principles of its original intent.

But the intent of the electoral clauses must always remain intact as the guaranteed right to the states by the Tenth Amendment doctrine.

In our history, we have seen political candidates early on tried to undermine our system because of their defeated loss. Indeed, more now in modern times where we have seen this travesty.

As you will see in the chapters of this book that I explore four elections that had a major impact in our union's constitutional form of electoral law and structure. Two in our history and two in our current history in where people tried to undermine our state (presidential) elections. Just because they lost their elections by a wide electoral vote margin, it does not give this candidate or group to claim "fraud." In a presidential election, it is the electoral vote, chosen by each state legislature to elect the chief executive of this union of sovereign states.

In today's current situation, left-wing progressives and right-wing nationalists have taken the liberty to take away our "republic" liberty from us in the shape of "democracy" to undermine our founding principles when it comes to our electoral structure.

We have seen people claim the idea of populism and a people's "right to vote." We have seen this idea come up with the indoctrination of populist democratic values. This union was never established to be a sort of a populist democracy. We have been established and to this day have been a representative American republic of sovereign and independent states.

A vote is not a right but a privilege. It has been a privilege given to the protection and regulation of each State, not of the federal government. It has been since the adoption of this nation in 1776. But unfortunately, in 1868, the national Congress passed an amendment to the Constitution guaranteeing the "right to vote" to all its citizens. This amendment happened just after a bloody civil conflict and the national government had to step in to claim this enforcement protection.

Now all citizens of this union have the right to vote in their state elections, there is no dispute about it. But the regulatory and enforcement lies within each state of this union. Now everybody has the right to vote, but with each vote comes the responsibility of each voter to vote accordingly and follow the instructions of that voting standard. That voting standard is set by each individual state's state legislature.

You will read in a couple of elections that people were disputing for their vote to be counted after they had exercised their right to vote. If the voter exercised their right to vote appropriately but their ballot did not follow the proper voting standard, then that ballot is not to be counted. Now a ballot must never go unrecognized due to the voter's race, sex, ethnicity, national origin, and sexual orientation. Those issues have been affirmed by Congress's 1965 Voting Rights Act. But despite these new issues added to this national act and guaranteed by the Fifteenth Amendment. Sovereign states still have the power to regulate and enforce their state elections, including in the general presidential election.

Just because a sovereign state's legislature redraws legislative maps and changes its electoral voting standards procedures. It does not mean that they are trying to undermine a certain voting block of people. People today are trying to prove discriminatory intent, but none have been proven as you read across this book.

Then we will see in recent elections in where we see in past and modern times where a candidate refuses to concede an election. We have seen it many times, but in the end, past candidates gracefully accept defeat and moves on with their life. But this will be the first time in where a presidential candidate refuses to accept defeat and because of his narcissistic ego pulls this republic further into an abyss of destruction to a centralized form of electoral governance.

Candidates must recognize their electoral defeat because it is so written in the Constitution. Each state chooses their electors and procedures in how to elect the chief executive. For a public official or a private citizen to undermine these state's procedures should be discouraged and be abhorred as we write the books in our nation's history.

To use one branch of the General Government of the United States to undermine a state's electoral codes and laws is tyrannical and unconstitutional. You will read in this book on multiple elections in where losing candidates tried to apply one state's electoral code from one state to fit his narrative. In both instances, both cases were dismissed and ruled in favor of the state's electoral clauses.

"Our consideration is limited to the present circumstances, for the problem

of equal protection in election processes
generally presents many complexities."

(Per Curiam of Bush v. Gore, 2000).

You will read in this book that there are complexities to this state's right of enforcement. These
complexities must be defined at the state level, not
at the federal level. Except when discussing the
Fourteenth Amendment.

You will read that even the three most liberal
jurists of the high court understand the rules of federalism when discussing the Fourteenth Amendment
and barring a candidate for federal, state, or local
office. Those liberal jurists do not deny the powers
of the sovereign state to bar a candidate from running
for office. They recognized the federal power and
state power when it comes to regulate elections.

The Fourteenth Amendment is a federal government tool to enforce a controversial candidate to bar
anyone from holding office. While the states have the
electoral clauses to enforce to bar a controversial candidate from running for office. That is the differences
of federal and state power not to coincide, intrude, or
contradict with one another as stated in our American
rules of federalism.

As you will see in this book, as I will explain how
the General Government of the United States from
their executive branch, national Congress, and high
court have undermined and put down this sovereign
State right. They have begun to draw federalization
of our state elections into a national standard by way

of Congress or by the courts. Whether it is a left-wing progressive or a right-wing nationalist, they are trying to create unified system that our union has never been set up for that type of centralized autocracy.

Many people have not heard of the Independent State Legislature theory, or that is what the liberal progressive movement calls it to be a thorn against the rose of the federalism. The Independent State Legislature Reality rule is very much alive and a true aspect of our constitutional way of life. It is stated in the electoral clauses of the federal Constitution, granting the power of the State *Legislatures*, that power to regulate and enforce elections.

As far as using the proper judicial review on an electoral law, it is only necessary and proper to study and debate the law in question. I believe that it is the court's duty on these matters to send back the law in queue to the *legislature thereof*, for review. It is not the court's job on these questions for the court to dictate judicial 'legislative' review and change or repeal the law. This is what I like to call undermining our electoral clauses and losing the sense of liberty to our sovereignty of each State.

I know many individuals have asked me why I did not include the 1860 election. 1860 was a serious election to our union's history but not as constitutionally drastic as the ones that I am going to detail in this book. I do not treat 1860 any different, even though this election is what drove this nation into a bloody conflict, but it is the first one that showed its true rules of federalism and states' enforcement of the electoral clauses.

Southern states had every right to place voting standards and remove candidates (Abraham Lincoln) from their ballot. And northern States also had that same right to remove candidates (John D. Breckenridge) from theirs. It is not like they were going to win those electoral votes, so what would it matter. States have that right to enforce their voting standards and procedures as they see fit. This is the reason, why I do not include this election in my book. This is one election that candidates did not show resentment at the state level. While only showing resentment at a federal level is a different analogy. The enforcement remained at the state level.

This book is to detail how this nation's electoral voting standards and procedures are established within each State. The purpose of the federal government is to be the administrator, not the regulator. Each state is to be the regulator of their elections, without infringing on the person's right to vote. Especially on account of their race, sex, or any form of identity.

This book aims to prove that the sovereign and independent States have every right to enforce their electoral standards.

When it comes to judicial review on reviewing states' electoral legislation. It is quite simple, it is supposed to be considered judicial review, not judicial 'legislative' review. The federal government's high court is to act like the administrator to review the case. If there are any unconstitutional aspects of the state's electoral law, then it should be remanded back to the state legislature for further review to be amended or repealed. It is not the job of the general government's high court or state court to act like the legislature. Especially when dealing with the electoral clauses.

I hope you will enjoy reading this book as I have enjoyed writing it. Explaining the role of the state legislatures in drawing up their electoral codes and standards while the federal government stands as the administrator.

If this republic and its current leaders live up to the guaranteed promises written by our Constitutional framers, then we all can live in a prosperous and liberty union.

I also want to touch base on the recent election our republic just had on November 5, 2024. I will continue to make this statement that this union was built by a unity of sovereign states, and not by a populist centrality of dependent states. Regardless what Donald Trump or Kamala Harris or any other federal government insider, America is not a democracy.

We should not and will not rely on a popular vote to decide our chief executive elections. We should always rely on our Constitution and electoral clauses that grant this power to this unity of sovereign states.

With how our republic is going and this scourge of Trumpism is hovering it, it will be difficult to return to a normalcy era of tranquil American republic. But I will keep on praying and supporting, we shall return to a peaceful American republic of sovereign states.

1824 Election

Article I, Section IV, Clause I

"The Times, Places and Manner of holding Elections for
Senators and Representatives, shall be prescribed in each
State by the Legislature thereof; but the Congress may at
any time by Law make or alter such Regulations, except as
to the Places of chusing [sic] Senators.

Article II, Section I, Clause II

"Each State shall appoint, in such Manner as the Legislature
thereof may direct, a Number of Electors, equal to the
whole Number of Senators and Representatives to which
the State may be entitled in the Congress: but no Senator
or Representative, or Person holding an Office of Trust or
Profit under the United States, shall be appointed an Elector.

In all the elections in American history, the election of 1824 was the one that was heavily crowded. There were candidates from across this great republic competing to promote their agenda. As stated in the prologue, this would be the first election in the post-Framers world. The principles of the Framers, in my own opinion are set in principle and need to be set for future generations of federalism to follow them. But unfortunately, new political ideas began to flourish with greater enthusiasm to dissolve the Framers' ideas. A flood of different political ideas flourished the American political scene and not one truly represented the principles of the Framers.

This election not only shows a wide variety of candidates of different political ideologies and background. I will demonstrate that it was an eye-opening question that not only this country can have multiple candidates running for president. The final constitutional deciding factor process is the electoral votes and heads to the national House of Representatives for its certification.

I rather have multiple candidates running for president than just two. With five or more, the competition and choices become clearer for the state electors, than just two.

This was not the last of elections with multiple candidates. But certainly, it was the last to follow its constitutional procedures. This election was decided appropriately by the national House of Representatives, and not by the court or by a federal government electoral commission. The constitutional procedure was not decided because of a strong populist sentiment.

But for some reason, many political pundits, past, and present have convinced the American people and other individuals to fear in sending an undecided election to the U.S. House of Representatives. Populism is what brought forth this idea. Populism crushes this republic into a sense fear for democratic tyrannical unprincipled policies. This is what we have seen in future elections, and this present, upcoming one in 2024.

Let us discuss the candidates of 1824 and see how they shaped this election and future elections.

The Virginia candidate offered a platform of centralization of a national power. That did not sit well with a few southern states but especially not with South Carolina. South Carolina, a young colony, became well-known for its admiration of state dependency off the federal government. Many historians of today deny this fact and want to place a different light towards the southern states.

South Carolina politician John C. Calhoun did not appreciate, later in his life, the politics of William Crawford. Calhoun as a then-young congressman championed the same ideologies as Crawford. For example, the tariff act of 1816 and the second bank of the United States.

William H. Crawford, a respectable bureaucrat of federal government means seems to have been the likely candidate to be president. He was Secretary of the Treasury under James Madison and James Monroe. To me, he seemed favorable because he was a long-standing member of the federal government and that is what the federal government sought to keep their friends close, but not their enemies closer. It is fortunate that he served under our Father of the Constitution, but his politics did not coincide with Mr. Madison.

He was one of the proponents of the establishment of the Second Bank of the United States. At this point in our early times of our republic, there was a fast, growing sentiment favoring nationalist governance rather than state sovereign governance.

"Under Chief Justice John Marshall, the Supreme Court had begun to deliver interpretations that favored the nation rather than states' rights. In *McCollough v. Maryland*, (1819), it even upheld the national bank's constitutionality in words borrowed from Alexander Hamilton, thus accepting both the principle of broad construction and a moneyed institution that the Republican Party had originally regarded as anathema. In the 1821 *Cohens* case, Virginia itself was sued in the Supreme Court "as a party in her sovereign capacity as a State, notwithstanding the provision in the Constitution that no State shall be sued." (The One-Party Presidential Contest: Adams, Jackson, and the 1824's Five-Horse Race, Donald Ratcliffe, The Virginia Candidate, page 31, Donald Ratcliffe, University of Press Kansas, 2015).

John Marshall, appointed by a framer to the constitution, was one of the main perpetrators with the assistance of Alexander Hamilton that began to ruin this wonderful creation of an American republic. More high court cases came about to place restrictions on the sovereignty of the States and embrace a national interest. One that they forgot to mention was *Gibbons v. Ogden*, 1824, in where a New York state law was found invalid under the constitution's commerce clause. It denied a state that could not deny any ships entering New York's port of entry and conducting business. The Commerce Clause is one heavily disputed and debated clause within the constitution.

Just a short note, on my constitutional opinion on how to define the Commerce Clause. Since the inception of this republic's first Constitution and later with the second Constitution, the interstate regulatory and enforcement of commerce is and will always be between the sovereign States. The General Government of the United States was to always act as the administrator of the States, but never the regulator, nor the enforcer. The way the Commerce Clause is written as "[The Congress shall have the Power] To regulate Commerce." Again, if you would know the writings of the framers, they never intended to use the word "regulate" as "control" or "enforcement." So, the Marshall court and future courts have totally misinterpreted this clause and its original concept.

The first generation of heirs to the framers knew that this was a form of aggression and encroachment towards the sovereignty of the States. The first generation of the Framers' heirs spoke out against the form of aggression for centralized national power. Unfortunately for the second, and at present-day generations to our framers have been completely lameducks towards this continuing aggression.

I do believe this election of 1824 was the light to shine against the turn on centralized autocracy. The electors and people started to look at candidates to reshape what the original framers intended to build this republic as stated not only in the constitutional convention but at the declaration of independence.

Different states had various opinions on how the general government needed to behave and operated.

"Many leading Virginia spokesmen for federal action, however, like the Federalist congressman Charles Fenton Mercer, opposed protective tariffs." (The One-Party Presidential Contest: Adams, Jackson, and the 1824's Five-Horse Race, Donald Ratcliffe, The Virginia Candidate, page 45, Donald Ratcliffe, University of Press Kansas, 2015).

"The state (South Carolina) had a long tradition of favoring nationalist policies." (The One-Party Presidential Contest: Adams, Jackson, and the 1824's Five-Horse Race, Donald Ratcliffe, The Virginia Candidate, page 47, Donald Ratcliffe, University of Press Kansas, 2015).

There is no dispute from me on the role for taxation in the federal government. The general government can establish any form of taxation if it is done in the form of indirect taxation and it causes no financial damage, or harm, or dependency towards the states.

This was the beginning age of either having centralization or individual powers. As we have seen prior to this election, the over-growing, unconstitutional sentiment of a national government.

Unfortunately, as new territories were entering into this constitutional compact of union of sovereign States. Many states were pondering on the slavery question.

"Looking to 1824, Adams privately told Plumer, "The question of Slavery in the new States—a President from the slave or free states—would in his opinion, be the great rallying point at the next election, &, of course render it a struggle between the north and south." (The One-Party Presidential Contest: Adams, Jackson, and the 1824's Five-Horse Race, Donald Ratcliffe, University of Press Kansas, 2015, A Northern Man, page 48).

Then came the Missouri crisis in where new territories were being discovered and forming new states into this American union of sovereign States. The slave-holding states wanted to keep their compromise alive as it was stated within the constitution, the three-fifths (unholy) compromise. While the non-slave-holding states wanted to end this unholy compromise and be rid of the hard-labor production known as slavery.

Slavery has always been the governing talking point of every single early nineteenth century election. Then came the talk of equality and civil rights in the late nineteenth century to the early parts of the twentieth century.

Eighteen-twenty-four was the turning point of our nation's beginning history. America had just survived a foreign invasion, coping in entering the world's stage with new economic trade policies as well as protective defense policies. Also, America was discovering new lands in the western frontier and the discussion led to these new territories entering this compact as free or non-free states of slavery. Nowadays, instead of just discussing about it, we resort to violence and aggressive actions instead of just discussing the affected issues.

This led to a vast political discourse that opened the flood gates later but 1824 directed us to open the issue of slavery and the new states.

In the 1820s, the high court of the land ruled that a New York state law was considered unconstitutional. The law was supposed to ban the sale and importation of human beings into the slave market. I abhor the very idea of slave labor because it weakens the human's morale and character. But I also abhor the arrogance of the general court in interfering in the independence and sovereignty of an American state.

I also do abhor the arrogance of the sovereignty of states of inputting their own illogical slave labor laws and anti-slavery laws onto others.

"Then in February 1844 the Ohio general assembly passed resolutions calling on the federal government to pass a law—with the consent of the slaveholding states—freeing at the age of 21, and then colonizing, all slaves born after the passage of the act. The resolutions declared that because "the evil of slavery is a national one," the people of all the states should share the costs. Seven other Northern states plus Delaware rapidly endorsed the proposal." (The One-Party Presidential Contest: Adams, Jackson, and the 1824's Five-Horse Race, Donald Ratcliffe, University of Press Kansas, 2015, A Northern Man, page 51).

State legislatures of the individual, independent, and sovereign states have a right to petition the national government for a better life, liberty, and the pursuit of happiness. But we should all remember that we cannot cross that sovereign state boundary because once we do; we go from a republic union of sovereign States to a democratic union of dependent States.

Slavery can be and was a national issue, but that does not mean that most of our sovereign States must bear the cost to any policy at the expense of another state or by the national government. The federal government was never established and continues with the same principle not to act as the giver of privilege. But neither the state government were granted this sense of privilege to their citizens.

Governments are not here to establish acts of charity but acts of law and justice. As 1824 begins to give charitable acts by the national government, we still see the same actions throughout our nation's lifetime and into 2024. I love charitable acts to offer compassion towards our fellow humans, but not at the expense of a citizen being forced by an aggressive general and/or state government.

1824 was an eye-opening towards the new federalism policies imposed by the first Framers' heirs. Some still maintained the same principles with the new policies. Others were wishy-washy to appease to the federal government master and cut away any independence to our sovereign States.

John Quincy Adams, the New England man had tendencies just like his father, but he was not as straightforward as his father on political promises, in my opinion. Quincy Adams wanted the approval of most of the states to obtain the nomination of his party and by that he tried to appease favor even with some southern allies, John C. Calhoun. He needed to curtail favor towards the New York state delegates and as you know well, New York at that time is the Florida of today.

Now comes the new era of America, the western frontier future. The man at the center of this new era but with its founding principles was *Henry*

Clay. Born in Virginia but raised in a new state, the Commonwealth of Kentucky.

"As a native Virginian who had moved to Kentucky, he enjoyed, in Adams's phrase, "that clannish preference which Virginian has always given to her sons." He had been recognized as a stout defender of states' rights through the Missouri crisis, and he could speak persuasively of maintaining the federal balance." (The One-Party Presidential Contest: Adams, Jackson, and the 1824's Five-Horse Race, Donald Ratcliffe, University of Press Kansas, 2015, The Western Interest, page 95).

"No other candidate so publicly committed himself to the package himself to the package of policies that Clay himself soon call the American system." (The One-Party Presidential Contest: Adams, Jackson, and the 1824's Five-Horse Race, Donald Ratcliffe, University of Press Kansas, 2015, The Western Interest, page 95).

I feel that Henry Clay had a dream for a non-egotistical American republic system, not a nightmare for a self-narcissistic ego American system. I would have most definitely would have voted for Henry Clay for president and if there are similar candidates today with the same American republic common sense, he or she got my vote. But, unfortunately, for today's political campaign world, there are none with the same founding principles as Clay.

"It is time that western men had some share in the destinies of this republic, St. Louis Enquirer, 1819." (The One-Party Presidential Contest: Adams, Jackson, and the 1824's Five-Horse Race, Donald Ratcliffe, University of Press Kansas, 2015, The Western Interest, page 97).

Ironically is that as America kept expanding towards the West, leaders that arose from that area, for some reason kept those constitutional founding principles from the Framers. Western Americans tended to be more constitutionally principled than Eastern Americans. They are more self-conscious of the money being spent nationally towards the sovereign States than the Eastern establishment Americans.

"These hopes achieved little success before 1824. Congress agreed in 1820 to locate the route of the national Road from Wheeling, Virginia to Indianapolis, but no money was forthcoming to build it. Congress even refused to vote money to repair the Eastern sections of the road: when in 1822 it passed a bill authorizing the erection of tollgates on the road to pay for repairs, President Monroe vetoed it on constitutional grounds. Then in December 1822 the Speaker of the House, Philip Barbour of Virginia, appointed a House committee on the National Road that was overwhelmingly hostile to the project, with not a single member from Maryland and Ohio, "the States principally interested." (The One-Party Presidential Contest: Adams, Jackson, and the 1824's Five-Horse Race, Donald Ratcliffe, University of Press Kansas, 2015, The Western Interest, page 98).

"Westerners could conclude only that they were seriously disadvantaged by Eastern political control. Western states suffered the financial disadvantage of not being able to tax federal lands either before purchase or for five years after." (The One-Party Presidential Contest: Adams, Jackson, and the 1824's Five-Horse Race, Donald Ratcliffe, University of Press Kansas, 2015, The Western Interest, page 98).

Because of new states entering this compact drew hard competition and harsh criticism from the Eastern, northeastern, and southeastern states. But just because Congress was being controlled by the Eastern establishment, does not mean that privilege and taxable compensation must only apply to the eastern states. All states must be treated equally, and no state shall be subject to a privilege status by the national government.

"Public programs required a change of heart at Washington, but at least the recent influx of settlers into the West promised that change must come soon. Western politicians prophesied in 1820 that their strength was "growing too mighty to be treated with contempt" because "the next census shall have given us our full share in the national government." (The One-Party Presidential Contest: Adams, Jackson, and the 1824's Five-Horse Race, Donald Ratcliffe, University of Press Kansas, 2015, The Western Interest, page 99).

"Kentucky was united in its attitude not only to federal economic policy, but also to the federal judiciary. U.S. circuit courts pronounced unconstitutional not only Kentucky's debtor laws but also the state's occupying-claimant laws, which protected the interests of actual settlers against those who claimed title of their land. In *Greene v. Bible* in 1823, the U.S. Supreme Court sustained the circuit court's condemnation, thereby provoking great hostility to federal judicial interference and calls for repeal of the 1789 federal judiciary act." (The One-Party Presidential Contest: Adams, Jackson, and the 1824's Five-Horse Race, Donald Ratcliffe, University of Press Kansas, 2015, The Western Interest, page 101).

The entry of a sovereign state to this constitutional compact of a republic shall never be united in attitude to appease the federal government. Kentucky separated from Virginia to form its own sovereign entity for new (western) adventures to enlarge this republic of sovereign and independent states. They enlarged our nation without the sphere of influence and spending from the general government. But unfortunately, there was an individual in American history that was extremely arrogant in his broad thinking in how to develop our republic away from its true constitutional principles and into a dependent and overpowering centrist nation. The sad thing is that he made you believe he was for those framers' principles. But he was just to get that popular voting sentiment support.

"Yet others saw that there remained one controversial substitute: another Western candidate, the one with an impressive military reputation, whom the Southwestern states had already taken up: Andrew Jackson." (The One-Party Presidential Contest: Adams, Jackson, and the 1824's Five-Horse Race, Donald Ratcliffe, University of Press Kansas, 2015, Enter the General, page 112).

Instead of the people in being unselfish with their decisions and look up to the politician's intellectual status, they look upon very selfishly the populist celebrity status of the politician. Even though, 2024 shows no politician with an impressive military reputation, it shows a tragic egomaniac narcissistic reputation, worse than any military hero.

When looking up to the future of the republic, we the States, respectively the people must look above any partisan gain and look for principle gain.

"Andrew Jackson did not stand for states' rights or the destruction of strong federal institutions and economic policies." (The One-Party Presidential Contest: Adams, Jackson, and the 1824's Five-Horse Race, Donald Ratcliffe, University of Press Kansas, 2015, Myth and Reality, page 5).

Andrew Jackson did not stand up for anything remotely to the principles of this republic. He only stood for himself and to satisfy his brutish and ill-mannered narcissistic ego. The Andrew Jackson tyrannical persona represents every single politician in pre-civil war and post-civil war eras, except for Cleveland and Coolidge.

"Genl. Andrew Jackson. The mirror of Washington. A Chief in All the Ways of the Battle Skill'd, Great in Council, Mighty in the Field." (The One-Party Presidential Contest: Adams, Jackson, and the 1824's Five-Horse Race, Donald Ratcliffe, University of Press Kansas, 2015, Enter the General, page 113).

Just because one man is a mighty tactician does not make him a leading man to lead our American republic of sovereign States. How people can be easily misled by a narcissistic ego-maniac unconstitutional individual. Only because he or she appears to have a golden voice, does not mean their policies are filled with golden promises. They are quite the opposite, and, in the end, they will disappoint you. The one that will suffer is the republic.

"On both occasions, Jackson showed scant regard for civil authorities, asserting the superiority of his personal judgment as commander on the spot. When Congress decided to investigate Jackson's behavior in 1818-1819, numerous junior army officers—"his suite"—turned up in Washington, thuggishly announcing their presence in the streets." (The One-Party Presidential Contest: Adams, Jackson, and the 1824's Five-Horse Race, Donald Ratcliffe, University of Press Kansas, 2015, Enter the General, page 114).

The arrogance of one will be pursued and discovered by the ethical truth of others. Tyrant Jackson, as I like to call him, he is not worthy to be titled President of these sovereign American States. If only the American state electors would have seen how this individual behaved, he would have never been electorally elected to be president in 1828 and again in 1836.

This was the beginning of the end of our glorious American republic as we entered the foundation days of tyrannical national executive governance. With the introduction of Andrew Jackson, dark days would begin to gloom over our sovereign States. New dark days would hover us that in the end, we would not been able to recover for future generations. Not only we saw a tyrannical form of national executive power, but we also saw a form of autocratic congressional rule and radical supreme court full of unconstitutional edicts.

"He refused to take the talk of the presidency seriously; apparently in 1821 he angrily declared, "I can command a body of men in a rough way; but I am not fit to be President."" (The One-Party Presidential Contest: Adams, Jackson, and the 1824's Five-Horse Race, Donald Ratcliffe, University of Press Kansas, 2015, Enter the General, page 114).

If only he would have taken this quote seriously. Then our union of sovereign States would have survived the unconstitutional wrath of Jackson.

"Many people had developed a negative view and had come to see him as a potential destroyer of the republic." (The One-Party Presidential Contest: Adams, Jackson, and the 1824's Five-Horse Race, Donald Ratcliffe, University of Press Kansas, 2015, Enter the General, page 116).

"Jackson's military glory did more than just satisfy national pride." (The One-Party Presidential Contest: Adams, Jackson, and the 1824's Five-Horse Race, Donald Ratcliffe, University of Press Kansas, 2015, Enter the General, page 129).

Those who fail to acknowledge the constitutional founding federalism principles of our republic will surely be the destructive force, whether a citizen or a politician. I see no glory and pride for Jackson's presidential legacy. Quite frankly, any chief executive that praises a tyrant, behaves like a tyrant, and acts like a tyrant, loses all credibility and legacy to be remembered as a leader of our American republic.

As I see that Andrew Jackson was the primary abyss of the fall of our glorious republic. Many successors will get to claim this title at post haste.

It is sad that many private citizens as well as their state electors did not see the lying behind these shady candidates turned into politicians. When they finally saw their deception, it was too late, and the damage was already done to the republic.

"Man is, indeed, ignorant of the future; nor was there a stronger illustration of the observation than is afforded by the result of that election!" (Against the Force Bill, by John C. Calhoun, 15 & 16 February 1833).

Calhoun, which he was one of the first supporters of Andrew Jackson to the presidency, later turned out to be one of the first disappointments towards the Jackson presidency. It is like former Vice-President Michael Pence towards the Trump presidency. But in this case, it took Pence a little more time to be convinced of the evils of one president that it took Calhoun. For some reason, the level of disappointment towards Trump is not as aggressive and large as the one it was towards Jackson.

"In each of these cases, Donald Trump is pursuing and articulating an agenda that is at odds with the conservative agenda that we governed on during our four years. And that's why I cannot in conscience endorse Donald Trump in this campaign." (Michael R. Pence, former Vice-President of the United States, March 15, 2024).

The election of 1824 is looking like every post-election including its soon bicentennial of 2024. Where people begin to regret their vote for arrogance instead of for principle. As history repeats itself, instead of repeating for the good of the republic, its going from bad to worse to an evil force of a populist democracy.

But let us see how the 1824 campaign for the president in detail shows the similarities to every single election including this upcoming one, 2024.

The election of 1824, to me, in my opinion, is the first election in exchange of ideas in how this republic was going to be governed. We had different framers and framers' heirs install centrist autocratic policies and rulings against the sovereign States. While installing very minimal policies favoring all our sovereign and independent states as the Constitution prescribes.

The full electoral race of 1824 was filled with different type of candidates, some to install a nationalist centrist power over the states. And a few, to favor the sovereign States. The Western candidate, Mr. Henry Clay. Although from Virginia, he was raised in the outskirts of a former Virginia territory now turned into a sovereign state. He adopted those same ideals with the keen interesting phrase known as "The American System." John Quincy Adams, William Crawford, and DeWitt Clinton, all come from the same cloth of family elitist society of Washingtonian politics. And all together to spread the word of a bigger and more aggressive federal government. They all do not hide their affection for the enlargement of the national government of the United States. Then enter the victorious general into the campaign battlefield, Andrew Jackson. Because of his popular military achievements, people were blind sided towards his campaign policies and promises. Jackson claimed to state that he was "the people's candidate", a populist demagogue statement to win over the majority while crafting to establish himself into his upcoming national policy programs. Jackson had no interest in continuing the legacy of the framers. The only legacy he wanted to proceed was his own and establish it by the swift of his sword rather than of the mighty pen. And this individual sought to proclaim to become president and begin to ruin it with this presence. This person was not the valuable candidate to be titled President of this America republic of sovereign States.

There was only valuable candidate that I would indeed ask my state electors to cast their vote for president of this republic. In 1824, there was at least one viable candidate that believed in our republic's principles... Henry Clay. In today's America's, there are no candidates today that fits with these principles that built this republic, America!

Foreign and national centrist defense policies began to plague our American republic of sovereign States even before this election. They sought to bring this republic into the international stage of diplomacy and war. We did not foresee the foreign bureaucratic train wreck that we see today.

The Monroe Doctrine was an excellent piece of general government foreign policy: But modern progressives and war hawks have made it into a mockery. President James Monroe, the last president belonging to the founder's doctrine established this policy. This policy was to remind the European powers that every nation in the western hemisphere was free and independent from European control and that this republic would come to their aid if such an invasion would take place. The invasion would take place as economic sanctions or if that came to play, a show of American national military power.

The candidates of 1824 as much as the candidates of today would show their military might presence without showing any constitutional regard to the nation.

"Some Americans, including Jackson, believed that, if successful, the French invasion would lead to an attempt to reconquer the newly independent Latin American republics and threaten the security of the United States. A reimposed imperial regime might prove more menacing than that old Florida, so recently acquired, might once more become a base of racial terrorists and foreign meddlers. If Spain transferred ownership of Cuba to Britain or France, the whole Gulf Coast would be threatened." (The One-Party Presidential Contest: Adams, Jackson, and the 1824's Five-Horse Race, Donald Ratcliffe, University of Press Kansas, 2015, A Season in Washington, page 145).

That has always been the centrist mentality. To install fear onto its sovereign States entities and its people for a central military governance presence. There was never such a threat of Spanish meddling into these sovereign States.

"Others argued for Secretary of War Calhoun; Crawford's supporters said the threat was exaggerated and portrayed their man as the "peace" candidate." (The One-Party Presidential Contest: Adams, Jackson, and the 1824's Five-Horse Race, Donald Ratcliffe, University of Press Kansas, 2015, A Season in Washington, page 146).

In the view of the general government, any time there is an international dispute, the centrist mentality always escalates it out of proportion to install fear for the excuse to increase the size of the federal government and diminish the rights of the sovereign States. The controversial, unprincipled, unconstitutional espionage acts passed during two major world wars; the Cold War fiasco; and the so-called War on Terror.

The Monroe Doctrine: This here enters the major dilemma that truly plagues our republic. Where does the control of the national government begin and where does it end for the safety of the sovereign states?

It is not the general government's business to install fear for the safety of this union of sovereign States. It is the business of the general government to protect the integrity of its national governance. Its national governance does not extend for the protection of the states.

"Did Congress have the power to vote for money for roads and canals?" (The One-Party Presidential Contest: Adams, Jackson, and the 1824's Five-Horse Race, Donald Ratcliffe, University of Press Kansas, 2015, A Season in Washington, page 156).

"Has Congress the right to pass this bill?" (Against the Force Bill, by John C. Calhoun, 15 & 16 February 1833).

Is the role of the federal government to bribe states for national public works with their votes for the current administration or future one? The government of the United States is explicitly not here to be the privileged arm of one state or various ones at the expense and aid for the rest of the union. Furthermore, thus creating a policy of dependency across this nation leads to social unrest and welfare instability.

"Van Buren claimed to favor federal construction; but only if a new constitutional amendment gave the federal government the power;" (The One-Party Presidential Contest: Adams, Jackson, and the 1824's Five-Horse Race, Donald Ratcliffe, University of Press Kansas, 2015, A Season in Washington, page 156).

In theory and in constitutional reality, the federal government whether its Congress or the executive branch does not have the authority craft orders for national roads and canals. Just read the writings by President James Madison when he vetoed a national public works bill in 1816. The roads are left up to the sovereign States to work together under the administrative control of the general government. States are here to collect direct taxation revenue and pay their share to the national government. If they chose to instruct their legislature to do so in the first place.

Martin Van Buren when not dictating his private organization known as "the Van B Boys" (*Seinfeld* TV show reference) was in fact, dictating like a bully for national government patronage of national roads and canals.

Even years later, John C. Calhoun questioned the financial actions of the federal government on spending onto and against the states. In the beginning, Mr. Calhoun stood for his federalism principles but as his age progressed in life. He began to be a liability for the sovereign States and a profit for the national government.

I do not favor any policy for a federal construction policy on national public works, and if there was ever a constitutional amendment to this effect. Then it will unfortunately be constitutional but once again be unprincipled. The Constitution was never meant to favor the federal government in the sense to be the cash cow recipient for the states for national infrastructure.

"In theory, states' rights objections did not apply because the federal government was acting as a landowner rather than as a government." (The One-Party Presidential Contest: Adams, Jackson, and the 1824's Five-Horse Race, Donald Ratcliffe, University of Press Kansas, 2015, A Season in Washington, page 156).

It would be plenty of states' rights objections because again the federal government cannot act as the proprietor and the state its servant. I have never placed the role of the general government of the United States to be nothing more than the administrator and not the regulator.

"In his great speech at the end of March, Clay linked tariffs with federal internal improvements in a scheme of policy of national independence, mutual interdependence, and economic interchange that held together his vision." (The One-Party Presidential Contest: Adams, Jackson, and the 1824's Five-Horse Race, Donald Ratcliffe, University of Press Kansas, 2015, A Season in Washington, page 158).

"Here the bill faced determined opposition both from King and from Samuel Smith of Maryland, who happened to be the Chairman of the Senate Finance Committee. He viewed the word "Tariff" as having achieved a "cabalistic" power in the House "superior to all discretion of reason," and he saw his duty as restoring common sense." (The One-Party Presidential Contest: Adams, Jackson, and the 1824's Five-Horse Race, Donald Ratcliffe, University of Press Kansas, 2015, A Season in Washington, page 160).

As much as I admire Henry Clay for his vision of his American system for this American union of States. It could have been achieved without sharing one cent from the national government.

To obtain national independence only exists when the national government grabs the power from the sovereign entities and excels in it. Mutual interdependence is not the reason for the creation of this union. There is also a reason they are sovereign states, not dependent states. And they cannot be dependent from one another and from the national government.

The vision of economic interchange can co-exist within this union of sovereign states when they work together, as how the preamble states, "to form a more perfect union." It is the states who in the spirit of federalism "to form a more perfect union" is in having a successful union. It is not the job or the responsibility of the federal government to be the regulator of and for the states.

All these ideologies that were affected in 1824, is affecting America in 2024. Back then, the Hamilton progressives were trying to install a centrist form of federal government and they were received with resistance. But today, the newly formed progressives are continuing to install more centralized policies to keep enlarging the federal government, and today they are met with little to no such resistance from any side.

Here is where we enter the dark world of populism that led us to this federal government nightmare that we are enduring today. Because of the ambition of populist candidates is why we have now been accustomed to an over growing federal style of governance.

"Jackson himself believed a congressional caucus would fly in the face of the people's legitimate democratic aspirations: "Such is the feelings of the nation that a recommendation by a congressional caucus would politically damn any name put forward by it [*sic*]." (The One-Party Presidential Contest: Adams, Jackson, and the 1824's Five-Horse Race, Donald Ratcliffe, University of Press Kansas, 2015, A Season in Washington, page 150).

"But it has to be a democracy that's fair. This democracy is—I don't consider us to have much of a democracy right now." (Donald Trump on The Hill article by Brett Samuels, 09/17/23).

Since I do not admire a man like Andrew Jackson, I will hold his statement to the lowest of all American statesman standards. For a politician, or a citizen to establish America as a sacred ornament for democracy. It is like "a hand that held the dagger and struck it into the back of its framer." America has and till this day, was never established to have any democratic populist tendencies. America was born a representative republic. The progressives may try to change the procedures, but this nation will remain a republic forever.

Democratic populism is what kills a representative republic. The very thought of the creation of popular support and encouragement to dictate our federal executive branch is the reason the Roman Empire collapsed. And what sovereign states are doing to give more power to the people is having a strict contradiction to the founding principles of our republic. One thing is individual rights guaranteed in our Ninth Amendment, the other is popular rights. Individual and popular are two different things, not conjunct with the other.

"The three largest of the four upper South states had already conceded the election of presidential electors to the people, but in the Lower South the electors were still chosen by legislatures that were deliberately apportioned to favor the low country and its special interests." (The One-Party Presidential Contest: Adams, Jackson, and the 1824's Five-Horse Race, Donald Ratcliffe, University of Press Kansas, 2015, Legislators Take a Hand, page 206).

Once again, the main issue interests of slavery plagued this republic in 1824, like the plague interest issues of Trumpism in 2024.

"The determination of the South Atlantic states to preserve traditional structures arose essentially from their commitment to slavery. They needed to defend themselves, not so much against the threat of abolition from within the state, as to forestall the temptation for the popular majority to tax slave property inordinately and so prompt slave owners to release their slaves, which could be in no one's interests. Though this consideration was less pertinent in presidential elections, South Carolina and Georgia still retained legislative choices of electors, but in 1824 that did not prevent the accurate expression of the electorate's narrowing views on federal relations and national policy." (The One-Party Presidential Contest: Adams, Jackson, and the 1824's Five-Horse Race, Donald Ratcliffe, University of Press Kansas, 2015, Legislators Take a Hand, page 206).

Americans have been historically stubborn. And with that stubbornness, is what has caused many issues to carry that burden and cast a dark cloud into America's future. With the issue of slavery, it has been that dark cloud that was transformed into a dark hurricane that led to separate dark storms known as reconstruction and segregation. Stubbornness has come in different shape and forms throughout our history. And it affects federal-state relations with protective unconstitutional national policies.

From new national constitutional civil rights policies to unprincipled national tax and fiscal policies that have led to unprecedented and destructive situations in our country's history. Indeed, that stubbornness has led us to a sense of unnatural dependency financed by most of the states and orchestrated by the federal government.

"The conviction that Calhoun could be trusted to defend South Carolina transferred easily in 1824 to the slaveholding Jackson. The states' rights opposition led by former U.S. senator William Smith objected that Jackson had supported the protective tariff and federal internal improvements, which the South Carolina legislature was on the point of declaring unconstitutional; thus Jackson had conceded not only vital Southern economic interests but the only true ground of sectional defense, namely strict construction. This noisy little campaign in support of Crawford had relatively little impact: the presidency was not an issue in the elections to the assembly, and there was little opposition in the legislature to the Jackson-Calhoun ticket, which won 132-25." (The One-Party Presidential Contest: Adams, Jackson, and the 1824's Five-Horse Race, Donald Ratcliffe, University of Press Kansas, 2015, Legislators Take a Hand, page 208).

America has had the somewhat tendency to support populism over constitutionalism. John C. Calhoun, in the beginning happened to be one of our brilliant American framers' heirs scholars that turned out to have sold out to support the Tyrant Jackson. I see a similarity of Michael R. Pence being a good standing constitutionalist before selling out to the Cultist Trump.

"...as personal hostility to Calhoun, would ensure that states' rights men elsewhere refused to support South Carolina in the nullification crisis of 1832-1833." (The One-Party Presidential Contest: Adams, Jackson, and the 1824's Five-Horse Race, Donald Ratcliffe, University of Press Kansas, 2015, Legislators Take a Hand, page 208).

And then history repeats itself without the history books considering it into account. Calhoun, like Pence withdrew their support when they saw that these policies were a danger to our republic. But unfortunately, because of Calhoun's primary support of Jackson that later he discovered he had made an error. The state of South Carolina found it difficult to regain their trust towards their senatorial representation of John C. Calhoun during the crisis of federal-state relations known as the nullification crisis of 1832.

"In terms of overall electoral votes, Jackson (99) and Adams (84) were by far the two leading candidates, with Crawford (42) a distant third. Clay (37) was excluded from the "contingent election" that now became necessary, but he was nicely placed to enjoy playing kingmaker in the House of Representatives." (The One-Party Presidential Contest: Adams, Jackson, and the 1824's Five-Horse

Race, Donald Ratcliffe, University of Press Kansas, 2015, Legislators Take a Hand, page 228).

In terms of overall electoral votes, Trump (232) and Biden (306) were the only two leading candidates. Not a highly candidate contested election, the clear majority winner was the challenger, Joseph R. Biden. In 2020, there was no need to send this election to the national House of Representatives, like 1824. Reason behind it is that one candidate obtained the majority.

Even though presidential candidate Andrew Jackson obtained a significant number of electoral votes, but not the majority. And since there was no majority winner, then the election as prescribed in the national constitution goes to the national house of representatives.

Even though President Trump did not receive a majority of electoral votes. He is not entitled to bring forth a claim of irreparable harm to his election to the White House. And as we learned from a previous election, the courts are not here to decide on the outcome.

But of course, Jackson like Trump have a large narcissistic ego and could not fathom the thought of losing an election. And therefore, called the election "a fraud." Jackson later unfairly called the U.S. House of Representatives decision, "a corrupt bargain." The same goes for Trump calling "to stop the steal" election.

In 1960, after such a close election between John F. Kennedy and Richard M. Nixon. Nixon knew that this election was not meant to be and henceforth conceded with grace to the victor. Kennedy's 303 electoral votes beat Nixon's 219. A difference of 84 votes. The 2020 election was a difference of 74 electoral votes, and yet Nixon sided with dignity and grace to let the new winner enter the White House. But as we are comparing the 1824 and 2020 elections and soon the 2024 election to see if Trump will finally concede defeat or still call our American electoral college system, a fraud.

When somebody calls this last republic's faithful electoral institution's a fraud, you are calling our constitutional framers a fraud. By calling them a fraud, you are bringing down 237 years of accomplished and functioning work.

I am here to tell you that the American electoral college system works and neither a left-wing progressive intellectual nor a right-wing nationalist will tell me otherwise. The Constitution grants the power to the sovereign States to organize and regulate their elections. While it gives administrative and fair power to the national government, the national Congress for electoral administration, not regulation or restriction.

It worked well in 1800, 1824, 2000, and 2020, and will continue to work if people do not fall into gullible minds and enter into a populist abyss.

"Jacksonians could be confident of only five states: Pennsylvania, Tennessee, Alabama, Mississippi, and South Carolina. Adams could count on the six New England states, and Crawford on three Southeastern states (Virginia, Georgia, and Delaware). That left ten states initially uncertain. The maneuvers to capture the critical number of thirteen were potentially labyrinthine and opened the way to deep suspicion." (The One-Party Presidential Contest: Adams, Jackson, and the 1824's Five-Horse Race, Donald Ratcliffe, University of Press Kansas, 2015, The Corrupt Bargain, page 232).

Trump supporters could be confident of only two states: Florida and Ohio. Biden could count as well on two states: Colorado and Nevada. That left five states initially uncertain that eventually went to the column of Biden. Georgia, Pennsylvania, Michigan, and Wisconsin. Those states' electors saw their way through to cast their vote for Joseph R. Biden as stated in their Article II power.

"The historian Robert [V.] Remini described the outcome as the "Theft of the Presidency," but that does less than justice to the real significance of all the politicking." (The One-Party Presidential Contest: Adams, Jackson, and the 1824's Five-Horse Race, Donald Ratcliffe, University of Press Kansas, 2015, The Corrupt Bargain, page 232).

I have no faith in no American, whether a presidential candidate or an ordinary citizen to outright call an election, a theft. This individual Robert Remini, he may have very well have been a prominent historian of our times. As I researched in his literary curriculum, he is a man of little faith in our federalism republic. He was a man of emotional convictions rather than a man of true constitutional convictions.

Those who compel to write the goods of a tyrant cannot be compelled to write anything good or just. I have no interest in writing the life stories of Andrew Jackson, or an FDR, or a Donald Trump.

When individuals state unneeded opinions to the public regarding an election, it brings forth bitterness and contempt, not for the country but for the constitution. At all times in our nation's history, there were people believing in the role of the people within elections. The people cast no role in our elections unless it is being granted by the individual state legislatures. Till this day, no state legislature has granted the popular vote right to choose their electors or even for the chief executive of our nation.

"The danger was, as Hezekiah Niles warned, that "such an election may shake the union, for it is possible one may be chosen, whom the people can regard only in the light of a usurper." (The One-Party Presidential Contest: Adams, Jackson, and the 1824's Five-Horse Race, Donald Ratcliffe, University of Press Kansas, 2015, The Corrupt Bargain, page 229).

The only usurper in a highly contested election is the one who lost and refuses to concede. There is no reason a single election must disrupt the day-to-day activities and lives of our nation's sovereign states. An election is just a daily function in our daily American lives. Chosen Americans set their right to vote for their candidate of their choice, and those will triumph if their candidate wins the seat of office. Those who do not see their candidate win, it is the way of the world and not meant to be, so we move on and look to a better day for the future of our nation.

There is no usurp leader waiting in the halls of Congress because the Constitution does not grant it.

Considering the 1824 elections, no candidate obtained most electoral votes and henceforth the election is being moved to the national House of Representatives to be decided.

Considering the 2020 elections, one candidate did not obtain the electoral votes to win and henceforth the election was given to the other candidate to win.

Considering the future 2024 elections, we will see which candidate obtains most of the electoral votes. And let us hope there is no contempt or dismay for our nation's most principled document, the Constitution.

"In 1823 Mahlon Dickerson had warned that "the broad road to monarchy is left open by those who formed our Constitution, by neglect or by design." (The One-Party Presidential Contest: Adams, Jackson, and the 1824's Five-Horse Race, Donald Ratcliffe, University of Press Kansas, 2015, The Corrupt Bargain, page 229-230).

Those who do not utterly understand the rules of federalism that govern its founding principles, are the true dangers to our union of sovereign American States.

There is no neglect from our constitutional framers and the design was closed to perfection to be "a more perfect union of sovereign States." The one road our framers did not want to venture was a road to a monarchy. Given that was the same road they steered away in 1776.

Andrew Jackson did venture into a road to monarchy expanding unconstitutional and unprincipled roles for the executive branch of the national government.

Mahlon Dickerson and future ideologues like himself speaks with such high contempt of the framers while supporting a man that behaved more like a monarch than a public servant.

"John Sloane of Ohio was not the only congressman to see evidence in Jackson's disposition, common among military men, "to contemn [sic] the salutary agency of the law, and rely on the application of force, for affecting all objects." Who else, other than Cromwell and Bonaparte, had "dissolved the legislature of a sovereign State, and suspended the operation of all its laws"?" (The One-Party Presidential Contest: Adams, Jackson, and the 1824's Five-Horse Race, Donald Ratcliffe, University of Press Kansas, 2015, The Corrupt Bargain, page 232-233).

This was the first elections in where the most popular of all candidates appear to be the most dangerous. That must always be a red flag to avoid any popular candidates. American Republic ideologues studied the history of the Roman republic times and saw the dangers of a replica of a Julius Caesar. Hence why they were not casting their vote towards the likes of an Andrew Jackson.

[The Corrupt Bargain]: "These charges always lacked substantiation." (The One-Party Presidential Contest: Adams, Jackson, and the 1824's Five-Horse Race, Donald Ratcliffe, University of Press Kansas, 2015, The Corrupt Bargain, page 237).

[The Stop the Steal Campaign]: "These charges always lacked substantiation."

History does repeat itself. And those who fail to learn from history are doomed to repeat it. And unfortunately, they will take this nation down with them unless we the States stop them.

Conspiracy theories that hold no constitution-ality only damage the integrity of the constitution. As I stated earlier, these theories are only causing to bring dismay and chaos. It brings dismay and chaos not to the popular electorate but to the integrity of the state electorate.

"Then in 1824 the established democratic system ceased to work..." (The One-Party Presidential Contest: Adams, Jackson, and the 1824's Five-Horse Race, Donald Ratcliffe, University of Press Kansas, 2015, The Corrupt Bargain, page 257).

There was never any established democratic sys-tem in this here American republic. For the author of this book to ever hint this ever idea is disingenuous, infantile, and erroneous. This American republic may have presented the idea of a little democratic popular process in their elections, but it remains to this day, a very well-drawn republic. The dem-ocratic popular vote has created more damage than of the electoral college vote. Popular votes enhance the very idea of anxiety, frustration, and corrup-tion... look at what the Seventeenth Amendment has created for our several States. We do not want a national Seventeenth Amendment to extend to pres-idential elections.

In this republic, We the People have our repre-sentation in government in our individual state level and to even extent in the national congress level, the national house of representatives.

"The House election became the manifest warn-ing, as the masthead warning, as the masthead of the leading Jacksonian newspaper would have it in 1828:

"POWER IS ALWAYS STEALING FROM THE MANY TO THE FEW." (The One-Party Presidential Contest: Adams, Jackson, and the 1824's Five-Horse Race, Donald Ratcliffe, University of Press Kansas, 2015, The Corrupt Bargain, page 257).

This is the populist lie to appease to the masses. Unfortunately, it's lies work to please to the ego that they are defending. There is no power greater than the Constitution. To even suggest that any power stole an election is dishonest to say the least.

"Furthermore, the cry of corruption had the electoral merit of appealing to all the suspicions of men in power that had built up over the years of panic and depression. If there was an "era of corruption" (as the historian Robert Remini argued), it was not in the 1820s but had peaked in the heady days of speculation immediately after the war, when bankers, land speculators, and their legal associates had exploited control of government at all levels to line their own pockets. (The One-Party Presidential Contest: Adams, Jackson, and the 1824's Five-Horse Race, Donald Ratcliffe, University of Press Kansas, 2015, The Corrupt Bargain, page 256).

And to this day, the election of 1824 as well as the election of 2020 was decided justly and fairly by our national congress. Rumors are just rumoring of election theft that was spread by the losing candidacy of Jackson and Trump. There was never a clear sign of corruption or fraud brought upon to a court. No fraud has ever existed in discussing these elections and no one has brought forth credible evidence.

To learn from all our elections and future elections, we must rely on the Constitution first, party politics later. We cannot rely and put our faith on a candidate to place dishonest information onto the people. Lies and distrust from our candidates only paves the way to distrust our political system, not our principled document.

1876 Election

Article I, Section IV, Clause I

"The Times, Places and Manner of holding Elections for Senators and Representatives, shall be prescribed in each State by the Legislature thereof; but the Congress may at any time by Law make or alter such Regulations, except as to the Places of chusing [sic] Senators.

Article II, Section I, Clause II

"Each State shall appoint, in such Manner as the Legislature thereof may direct, a Number of Electors, equal to the whole Number of Senators and Representatives to which the State may be entitled in the Congress: but no Senator or Representative, or Person holding an Office of Trust or Profit under the United States, shall be appointed an Elector.

This was an election that was also set in the same year that was to celebrate this American union of sovereign States' centennial independence. It was very disappointing to see most Americans' behavior towards this election was a tragedy to see our nation celebrate its one hundredth year of independence.

Eighteen seventy-six was a very rebellious election for all since the southern states were re-admitted fully. This election paved a way of a new form of electoral administration turned into regulation that has created this democratic debacle of a mess we see today.

But I am not quite surprised that people behaved in this fashion in bringing some sort of populist resentment since 1824. In where people did not take lightly the results and really shown a bloody-self-image towards our Constitution and electoral clauses.

With Grant's first presidential election victory in 1868, it was likely that the Republicans were in control of the entire United States and its general government. The southern states that were finally re-admitted into the union were at a vulnerable state of mind. The radical Republicans in Congress were putting down the rebellious states into massive martial law control and helping the newly freed slaves entering the citizenship class of this nation.

In the 1868 elections, the son of the founder of the Republican Party ran for the 1868 Democratic vice-presidential ticket. We are starting to see a new wing of the republican party, known as the Liberal Republicans, trying to be in friendly terms with the southern states and its former confederate individuals.

"All joined a political revolt against Grant known as the 'Liberal Republican movement.'" (By One Vote: The Disputed Presidential Election of 1876, Republicans' Fall from Grace, Michael F. Holt, University of Press Kansas, 2008, page 2).

There were many prominent members of the Republican Party that were once members of the abolitionist movement and for a stronger union without the forced labor known as slavery. Such members like Massachusetts Senator Charles Sumner,

Ohio Congressman James M. Ashley, Pennsylvania's Civil War Governor Andrew Curtin, and incumbent Massachusetts Congressman Nathaniel P. Banks.

They steered away to throw their support towards President Grant in his 1872 re-election campaign, even though, Grant showed good numbers in the Midwest and some southern states.

"Yet federal military intervention and prosecutions in federal courts, authorized by a series of Enforcement Acts in 1870 and 1871, had effectively suppressed the Klan and preserved Republican control in most former Confederate states by the end of 1872." (By One Vote: The Disputed Presidential Election of 1876, Republicans' Fall from Grace, Michael F. Holt, University of Press Kansas, 2008, page 2).

"Republicans never dominated Virginia's state government, even though Grant carried it in 1872." (By One Vote: The Disputed Presidential Election of 1876, Republicans' Fall from Grace, Michael F. Holt, University of Press Kansas, 2008, page 2).

"Yet Republicans competitiveness in those states was precarious, indeed. By 1876, Republicans still dominated the governmental machinery in only South Carolina, Florida, and Louisiana." (By One Vote: The Disputed Presidential Election of 1876, Republicans' Fall from Grace, Michael F. Holt, University of Press Kansas, 2008, page 2-3).

And these were the three states that had issues with their electoral votes in deciding the election for Rutherford B. Hayes over James Tilden. These were three states that were heavily Democrat controlled before and during the Civil War. And yet, to ease of that control, Republicans issued tough legislation to place Republican state officials to give freedom to the newly freed slaves to participate in their new nation's citizenship status. The sad thing is that with that much participation of the freed-black citizens. They were the victims of several massacres including the one in Louisiana that led to a terrible high court decision that ban these citizens their guarantee of their second amendment right.

As the Democrats were easily gaining control back into the political life, they still did not have that total control they once had in pre-1861. So, they began to campaign for a Liberal Republican that was listening and showing guilty empathy towards them: Horace Greeley.

"Nor was Greeley popular with all Republicans sympathetic to the Liberal Republican movement. Whereas Liberal Republicans demanded a sharp reduction of tariff rates, Greeley had been a lifelong proponent of high protective tariffs. Nor did Greeley seem sympathetic to the Liberals' other top priority—civil service reform that would destroy party politicians' control over the federal government's workforce. By 1872, Greeley had embraced Liberals' demand for an end to federal intervention in the South and a restoration of full political rights to those former Confederates still disqualified from holding office by state laws and the third section of the Fourteenth Amendment." (By One Vote: The Disputed Presidential Election of 1876, Republicans' Fall from Grace, Michael F. Holt, University of Press Kansas, 2008, page 3).

Honestly, the disgraceful election of 1876 was the occurrence of a weakling party candidate in 1872 the led to major disagreements, turmoil, and chaos in that presidential election.

As my readers know from my writings that I do not and have never condoned any part of the 1861 secessionist movement. As Lincoln brought on that precedent before his unfortunate assassination and death of forgive and forget the southern states in rebellion. This led to future precedents to begin an appeasement promise to the rebellious individuals seeking a return of the American political life. And Horace Greeley began this movement that further enraged these former Confederate-Democrats into a wild rage entering 1876.

"The Liberal Republican movement, in short, did not simply fade away after Greeley's defeat in 1872." (By One Vote: The Disputed Presidential Election of 1876, Republicans' Fall from Grace, Michael F. Holt, University of Press Kansas, 2008, page 7).

Horace Greeley may have lost in 1872 against Grant, but that opened a wound of appeasement and forgiveness that led to violence and murder of thousands of citizens of the black-American race, circa 1876.

To gain populist sentiment from across the country, President Grant did a very disgraceful and distasteful thing that in the end caused dismay and chaos.

"To propriate the northern electorate's growing impatience with Reconstruction and the political warfare over it, Democrats in 1872 announced a "New Departure" by promising that they would no longer seek to repeal the Reconstruction program or the constitutional amendments. Echoing Liberal Republicans, Democrats said they wanted to move on

to different issues. Republicans tried harder to neu-
tralize the Liberals' appeal. At Grant's urging, congressional Republicans in 1872 passed an amnesty act
that removed political disqualifications from all but a
handful of former Confederate leaders, lowered tariff
rates by 10 percent, and repealed the income tax and
all excise taxes save for those tobacco and alcohol."
(By One Vote: The Disputed Presidential Election of 1876, Republicans' Fall from
Grace, Michael F. Holt, University of Press Kansas, 2008, page 8-9).

I am not surprised, and we should not be surprised
of every single politician selling out to gain more popular trust. It is ever so surprising to see a once great
general of the Civil War fight against the injustices of
slavery and a rebellious might of the Confederacy. To
see this man, betray the newly freed slaves that were
once in chains go back in chains by giving amnesty to
these treasonous rebels.

Ulysses S. Grant, a once great military official
was sharply reduced to a mediocre president. A
president that instead of holding on to his principles,
were immensely reduced to a point of selling out to
the very same individuals he fought a waged war
against them.

Grant's second term is the reason that the madness
of the 1876 election came about. Lincoln's promise of
forgive and forget finally came to a reality to offer
amnesty to these rebellious individuals.

Even though, Grant was in his second term, his
terms of office were of poorly and lame duck ones. Not
to mention that he endured a major scandal regarding

with the Union Pacific Railroad known as The Credit Mobilier scandal.

"...the Credit Mobilier was a construction company composed of the corporate directors of the Union Pacific Railroad. In their capacity as the railroad's directors, they hired the Credit Mobilier (that is, themselves) to build the road and readily paid its padded bills with the U.S. bonds Congress had appropriated to subsidize construction. Then, through the agency od Massachusetts Republican Congressman Oakes Ames, the Credit Mobilier supposedly bribed enough Republican congressmen by selling them its stock substantially below market value to delay a congressional investigation of the company's raid on the Treasury." (By One Vote: The Disputed Presidential Election of 1876, Republicans' Fall from Grace, Michael F. Holt, University of Press Kansas, 2008, page 9).

This happens when the general government of the United States begins to offer taxable funds for pet projects. The federal government was never meant to appropriate any funds for whatever reasons to the sovereign States or its citizens. It was especially not meant to use public funds for private interests. But with the arrogance that President Grant brought to the White House, the nation suffered plentiful arrogance with corruption. Plus, while they were stealing from the public coffers, the black-American citizens were beginning to suffer the wrath from the amnesty-liberated former Confederate individuals.

"To mobilize even more blacks for the Republican Party, Republicans passed civil rights laws in three states and gave more elective and appointive political positions to blacks. In short, Democrats simultaneously took up the mantle of white supremacy. They called on whites to restore "home rule" by driving the now black-oriented Republican machines from power. In this new situation, Democrats clearly had the advantage. Although black turnout for the Republican Party did in fact increase in some southern states, previous white abstainers for outnumbered blacks who had hitherto failed to vote. Consequently, in 1874 most remaining Confederate states where blacks lacked a majority of the potential electorate—Alabama, Arkansas, and North Carolina—also fell to the Democrats. Undoubtedly, the impending civil rights bill in Congress helped spark the movement of racist whites towards the Democrats." (By One Vote: The Disputed Presidential Election of 1876, Republicans' Fall from Grace, Michael F. Holt, University of Press Kansas, 2008, page 13).

"The upshot of this tug-of-war was that in April 1874 Congress passed what became known as the 'Inflation Act,' over the opposition of eastern hardearned-money men in both parties." (By One Vote: The Disputed Presidential Election of 1876, Republicans' Fall from Grace, Michael F. Holt, University of Press Kansas, 2008, page 16).

When Congress begins to invest their arrogant energy to control the financial and fiscal policies of the States and its citizens. There would be an uproar and disappointment in the next elections. Luckily, for President Grant, he vetoed a legislation of corrupt arrogant proportions to avoid an upset in the people's minds.

But fiscal and financial policies were affecting many individuals across the union but also it was affecting black Americans, when white supremacist Democrats were gaining in the popular voter rolls and gaining momentum once again in state and some federal offices.

"By mid-November 1874, in sum, Republicans knew that when the new Forty-fourth Congress met in December 1875, Democrats would control the House of Representatives for the first time since the mid-1850's." (By One Vote: The Disputed Presidential Election of 1876, Republicans' Fall from Grace, Michael F. Holt, University of Press Kansas, 2008, page 17).

As Jefferson once stated, this country needs to have peaceful revolutions every two years, they will be called elections. But unfortunately, the new wave of the Democratic Party fueled by anger from the radical Republicans after the war, and then given amnesty by the liberal Republicans were not going to achieve a full working congress majority by peaceful measures.

This happens every time, the party in power lusts for power to obtain it, And, when they obtained too much power, they began to sell out on their initial traditional principles that the other side will take advantage by any means necessary. This is what happened in 1874, and then the powder keg exploded in 1876.

"Democrats' white supremacist campaign in the South, fueled in part by anger at the impending civil rights bill, disgust at the corruption permeating the Grant administration—from Washington to local custom houses, navy yards, and internal Revenue offices—and most important, resentment of hard times, which found an obvious target in the incumbent majority party, all undoubtedly contributed to the Republicans' smashing defeat." (By One Vote: The Disputed Presidential Election of 1876, Republicans' Fall from Grace, Michael F. Holt, University of Press Kansas, 2008, page 17).

We all knew that these former and new Democrats were going to resent any legislation and Republican Party majority policies towards the newly freed black individuals made into citizens. We knew that they even tried to resist to not enforce the Thirteenth Amendment by several re-admitted southern state legislatures. These legislatures passed these "Apprenticeship Acts" that gave a new name to slavery. These acts across these Southern states forced the black American population head back to the agriculture fields, not by forced labor anymore. They were getting paid, very minimal, but you could say that it was again forced labor.

And yet, the Republican Party in control, to find appeasement towards these Democrat white supremacists, some members crossed the lines in the evil spirit of "bipartisanship" to ease up on the harsh reconstruction policies.

And because of that, we saw a major switch of power in the Halls of Congress. Democrats regained that control, they once had in 1850. History does repeat for the worst, and this is worse than 1861. 1850 is when Democrats passed a horrible piece of legislation that endangered the other sovereign

States and the rules of federalism governing our union. It was likely that we were going to return to these dangerous times after this unholy victory by these Democrats.

"Those elections produced one of the most stunning reversals in American history. In 1872 Republicans had captured 196 House seats and the Democrats only 83, with 2 southern seats won by Independents. In 1874 Democrats won 167 House seats and the Republicans only 99; in addition, 8 anti-Republican Independents won election." (By One Vote: The Disputed Presidential Election of 1876, Republicans' Fall from Grace, Michael F. Holt, University of Press Kansas, 2008, page 17).

"Democrats won the governorship and usually the legislative majorities as well in California, Missouri, New Jersey, New York, and, astonishingly, Massachusetts. Democratic gains in the states translated into Democratic gains in the Senate. Whereas Republicans had enjoyed a fifty-seat Senate majority over Democrats as recently as the Forty-first Congress (1869-1871), in the Forty-fourth their edge would be reduced to fourteen seats." (By One Vote: The Disputed Presidential Election of 1876, Republicans' Fall from Grace, Michael F. Holt, University of Press Kansas, 2008, page 17).

It is nothing out of the ordinary for the national Congress to have majority shift changes every two or four years, Congress has elections. But what it is sad that is that the party that is in control has a sudden shift of principles from traditional to liberal.

We have seen it in the nineteenth century, twentieth century, and even in today's elections. If the politician remains true to their word since the first time they got elected, those principles will keep them in office. If they lose is because of partisan popularity and against their state and constituent base.

You have had states where it has been predominately one political party in control, then lose it to the other political party. Take Massachusetts for example, where the Republican Party was a strong-hold electoral and popular state. Then the most popular national Senator, who was an advocate for the abolition of slavery. He decided to fight for amnesty and appeasement to the individuals that wanted to continue this abomination known as slavery. And with that, the sovereign State of Massachusetts went from Republican to Democrat.

It was like what happened to that same state in the 2009 midterm elections. That state had a seat controlled by the Democratic Party for years, till the death of that individual, then that seat was turned over to the Republican Party. It is a matter of change that is not needed but because of that party's holdover, the people and the state so desperately crave for a change. In a political party's takeover, the candidates will change, but the national directive policy promises remain the same. This change does not help the union but damages its federalism credibility.

We had something similar in 2017 and 2020 elections in Alabama. A senate seat went from Republican to Democrat at first, then Democrat to Republican, and the national directive policy promises did not change among these candidates.

"The Democratic vote in 1874 also clearly included Liberal Republicans who had voted for Greeley in 1872." (By One Vote: The Disputed Presidential Election of 1876, Republicans' Fall from Grace, Michael F. Holt, University of Press Kansas, 2008, page 18).

When there is a candidate that loses their party's traditional principles and moves on to newer principles, the constituency changes to appease to that candidate. This creates swing candidates and creates confusion.

It appears to me that this was the first time in American electoral history where we saw voting constituents flip from one political candidate to the other and remains with the same political atmosphere.

"To assert that the second session of the Forty-third Congress, sitting from December 7, 1874, until March 3, 1875, determined the outcome of the 1876 presidential election is an exaggeration." (By One Vote: The Disputed Presidential Election of 1876, A Pivotal Congressional Session, Michael F. Holt, University of Press Kansas, 2008, page 19).

Not only an election will change the political views of its constituent electorate but the way laws will be presented, debated, and passed. These similar laws will have a negative effect in the 1875 Congress, there will be laws and rulings affirming these laws that contradicted the Constitution and its rules of federalism.

These swinging elections did not amend only the presidential elections but future elections for complete chaos for the future of our union of sovereign States.

This was the beginning of political partisanship over constitutional principles. Even in 1860, there was no bickering over partisan politics, it was a discussion of constitutional principles and the issue of slavery.

Nowadays, after the civil war, we entered a world of party principles and which party must be in control and displace all constitutional value.

There was a reason that George Washington despised the idea of political parties. It is the very idea that ruins the very thought to unite to work and maintain this American union of sovereign States.

Enter the national Senator of Indiana Oliver P. Morton, Republican, the Ted Cruz of its day.

"On January 21, 1875, he reported a proposed constitutional amendment from the Committee on Privileges and Elections that would change the way presidents were elected. The debate on how to choose and count electoral votes would continue intermittently in the Senate for the remainder of this short session. The gist of Morton's proposed constitutional amendment was to have states elect all but two of their electors by congressional districts rather than by winner-take-all statewide slates." (By One Vote: The Disputed Presidential Election of 1876, A Pivotal Congressional Session, Michael F. Holt, University of Press Kansas, 2008, page 25).

Congress sets the date and times of a federal election. Congress has no authority to set the standard and procedures of a federal election for a sovereign state/s.

"Many Americans today would find this proposal appealing." (By One Vote: The Disputed Presidential Election of 1876, A Pivotal Congressional Session, Michael F. Holt, University of Press Kansas, 2008, page 25).

Only a true American will tell you, it is the independence of our sovereign States that keeps us free. A true American constitutionalist would repudiate and vote against this proposed attack on our Article I and II electoral provisions. But Americans today would probably be in joy towards this proposal because they have become more dependent off the federal government.

Federal presidential elections are quite distinct than state and local elections. It is comparing apples to oranges, because it is two different forms of electoral procedures and results.

"...as many predicted, New York's Democratic Governor Samuel J. Tilden (elected in 1874 by a comfortable, if suspicious, 50,000 popular majority) was the Democratic presidential candidate in 1876." (By One Vote: The Disputed Presidential Election of 1876, A Pivotal Congressional Session, Michael F. Holt, University of Press Kansas, 2008, page 26).

People may scream "Fraud!" and "Stop the steal!" about an election result; it is their first amendment right. But there is something called evidence to produce to present with your allegations.

Candidates win elections, candidates lose elections, it is a part of a healthy republic. But what is not healthy is anger and violence.

"How should Congress resolve cases in which states submit rival slates of electoral votes?" (By One Vote: The Disputed Presidential Election of 1876, A Pivotal Congressional Session, Michael F. Holt, University of Press Kansas, 2008, page 26). A question given by several members of the national Senate towards Morton's proposed amendment on elections. The answer is absolutely nothing. Congress is set to authorize the time and place for federal elections, not the manner of chusing the candidates. That manner is left up to the sovereign States embedded in the Article I and Article II power, and guaranteed by the Tenth Amendment.

Senator Morton of Indiana and other senators alike enjoyed bringing up fear stories and tactics upon the people and Congress. This happens when partisan politics takes the gavel over the Constitution.

"In 1872 Congress had refused to count the electoral votes from Louisiana and had come within a whisker of doing so in Texas, Mississippi, and Arkansas. But in 1872, Morton noted, those votes did not matter, for Grant had clearly won an electoral vote majority anyway. But what would happen, he ominously asked, if the electoral votes in question could determine the winner?" (By One Vote: The Disputed Presidential Election of 1876, A Pivotal Congressional Session, Michael F. Holt, University of Press Kansas, 2008, page 27).

It is not for Congress' job to show privilege or not to a state. Their job is to accept the electoral votes after they have been ratified by each of the state legislatures. Regardless if Louisiana casts its entire electoral votes towards the candidate, then so be it. But there should be no inquiries on the electoral votes that have reached the halls of Congress for verification.

But sadly, these inquiries are made at the height of political partisanship and bitter civil enemies and against the Constitution. Therefore, even at the height of the 1800 or 1824 disputed election, there was never any hint of political partisanship. At the end of the day, the individuals in this scenario, they respected everybody including the constitution and its rules of federalism.

"When electoral votes were counted in 1877, he warned, "the House will be Democratic and the Senate will be Republican." House Democrats were certain to reject enough electoral votes from Republican states so that no one had a majority. Then, according to the Constitution, the decision would be thrown into the Democratic House, which "will elect a Democrat for President." His warning culminated with the following rant:" (By One Vote: The Disputed Presidential Election of 1876, A Pivotal Congressional Session, Michael F. Holt, University of Press Kansas, 2008, page 27).

> "It will be in the power of our friends on the other side in the next House of Representatives...to throw the election into the House no matter what the votes may be. Under the rule the Republican party cannot elect a President. Why? Because it is in the power of the House of Representatives,...to throw out the vote of every Republican State...The result would be that the election would go into the Democratic House." (By One Vote: The Disputed Presidential Election of 1876, A Pivotal Congressional Session, Michael F. Holt, University of Press Kansas, 2008, page 27).

There is no room for party politics in this union. There is only room for constitutional politics. When you open the floodgates of party politics, then you give that entry to political games and schemes from both sides.

This was the first election that introduced party politics to gain control of others and disavowed the true principles of this American union.

To play party politics instead of constitutional politics is to head down a path of national government dishonesty and hypocrisy for future generations. Because of this congressional session, filled with political partisan hacks, from both sides, is the nation we have now at present times.

With the introduction in entering this heavily controversial 1876 election, the national Congress admitted new western states into this constitutional compact. With the admission of Colorado, Nevada, and Kansas, new electoral votes were added. Unfortunately, they were added in the ever scheme of party politics. In today's politics, there are no new federal territories to add into this union as states. What the General Government of the United States adds is more debt and dependency to the existing fifty sovereign States. But just as they added the states of Missouri and Maine, prior to the 1824 elections. But that was a compromise, unholy as it may seemed, it was not of playing party politics.

Grant, as General of the United States army was not an appeaser to get any rationale terms towards the rebel army of the Confederacy. He had no opinions to hold back to show that he wanted the Southern states in rebellion to pay for the start of the war.

But as he started to be closer to the dangers of central government, Washington City, he began to lose that good sense of principles, he once had. So, for the Democrats to install to be himself into a tyrannical force is way too far-fetched.

"Democrats, indeed, charged with "Caesarism," or plotting to undermine republican self-government." (By One Vote: The Disputed Presidential Election of 1876, Previews, Michael F. Holt, University of Press Kansas, 2008, page 34).

Is this the same Democratic Party that tried to undermine our federalism republic in 1850? By installing a national directive to pursue to persecute human beings while diminishing and denying the sovereign rights of other states, is very Caesarism, indeed. It is also very hypocritical at best in the world of politics.

The Republican Party were no saints in their own Roman Senate. They also acted quite tyrannical. President Lincoln was no saint. He ordered the removal of Habeas Corpus trials and introduced the first set of military tribunals.

Even the Confederate-style of federal government, in my opinion, were not Catonians but Caesareans. Jefferson Davis did not want to follow into the footsteps of Scipio. He was trying to install a southern version of a Washington style federal government.

This quote may or may not have some truth against Grant, but quite frankly, every president has had Caesarean characteristics.

This style of slander, whether truthful or untruthful, is when party politics gets chocked up in their own hypocrisy. We would not have to resort to these types of comments if all candidates for public office; federal and state, and politicians read and followed the Constitution as written with the newly added post-civil war amendments.

"In September, before leaving for the army reunion in Iowa, Grant had decided against sending troops to Mississippi in order to aid Ohio Republicans in the October 12 gubernatorial election." (By One Vote: The Disputed Presidential Election of 1876, A Pivotal Congressional Session, Michael F. Holt, University of Press Kansas, 2008, page 53).

"Moreover, Republicans had good reason to believe retaking Ohio from the Democrats was absolutely essential if they were to retain the White House in 1876. For these reasons, and because the Ohio story introduces us to the man Republicans would nominate for president in 1876, that story merits a separate chapter." (By One Vote: The Disputed Presidential Election of 1876, A Pivotal Congressional Session, Michael F. Holt, University of Press Kansas, 2008, page 53).

Political Parties are private institutions, and I could care less what goes on in their conventions and party procedures. But when the party in power uses their means and power in the hands of the national government at the expense of the public coffers, then we have a major problem.

The 1870s was indeed the beginning of a true two-political party partisan politics over constitutional politics. In the 1990s, this two-party system united to oust independent and third-party candidates and parties. This perfect dictatorship of a two-party system used to hate each other to finally unite to be hated by all. I rather not have political parties that create divisions and unifications. Those two parties, Republican and Democrat, have only created damages to our republic.

As the Roman Republic had a terrible civil war that led to civil unrest to unconstitutional imperialist regimes, so did our American republic. From multiple leaders deciding the fate of our republic.

I lost mistrust, not faith, in our American republic when they introduced Andrew Jackson to the American electoral scene in 1824. Then later an invasion of independent state sovereignty in the form of federal legislation to appease and offer privilege to the southern "slave-owned" states. I still believed there are still good American citizens that believed in our American federalism republic of sovereign States above any political party politics.

As I continually to analyze what led to the 1876 elections, and the future elections, I found much sadness for our ailing federalism republic.

As it brought me sadness in discussing the 1824 elections, 1876 is no different. The level of citizens from different states, not requesting, but demanding federal government aid and assistance is quite astonishing and tragic.

* * *

The Lincoln post-war policy began surging during the middle of Reconstruction by the once radical republicans in Congress that wanted the south to bleed for the start-up of the war. This policy that Lincoln introduced was the forgive-forget policy to the former Confederate states. Even General Grant repudiated this policy, but President Grant started to welcome it with open arms.

This is what happens when politicians spend too much time in the halls of the national government and sell out from their original principles.

And so, we enter Rutherford B. Hayes into the 1876 presidential race. A former military official like Grant. An Ohio man and that has a personal vendetta against the Confederate states.

This 1876 election race is an interesting race to me because it was on the Centennial year of independence. During that time, both sides of the political party spectrum had made a mockery of the independence fight that our framers had endured. The same goes for 1976, our bicentennial year, also was plagued by a similar mockery. Let us hope we will still have a republic in 2076, our tricentennial year. And no mockery or Trumpism will plague our republic.

Yes, by now the former Confederate states had been re-admitted back into our union. There were some that still wanted to bring back the old antebellum days and disregard the new policies passed in 1865 and 1868. It was those individuals that the Republican Party wanted to offer an olive branch and appeasement.

"All southerner's constitutional rights must be honored. I "shall labor for this end. Let me assure my" southern countrymen that my administration "will be one which will regard and cherish their truest interests—the interests of the white and of the colored people, both equally—and which will put forth its best efforts in behalf of a civil policy which will wipe out forever the distinction between North and South in our common country." (By One Vote: The Disputed Presidential Election of 1876, The Campaign, Michael F. Holt, University of Press Kansas, 2008, page 124).

All American's constitutional rights should be honored, of course, till that person has been convicted of a crime. Of course, all rights should apply to all citizens based on race. But sadly, from 1876 to even some present times, our citizen's rights have been violated on both sides of the race, more against black Americans than white Americans.

But I see that the radical republicans that once wanted the south to bleed, turned to show appeasement towards the south. But turns out that Hayes was more hypocritical than Grant. He promised his southern constituency, a return of constitutional rights but pondering if it should have been returned.

"Repeatedly, he privately wrote to Republican campaigners such as James Garfield, James G. Blaine, Oliver Morton, and Carl Schultz that "the true issue in the minds of the Masses is simply, shall the late rebels have the government?" (By One Vote: The Disputed Presidential Election of 1876, The Campaign, Michael F. Holt, University of Press Kansas, 2008, page 124).

* * *

The 1824 elections were the first elections in where a constitutional framer was not running, and new ideas came about during this time. But some of their ideas were of a federal government influence and aid towards the sovereign States.In 1876, it was the centennial birth of our union of sovereign States and yet the new individuals, that came out of an internal and idiotic bloody conflict still came my astonishment that require the same or different federal government aid and assistance.

The very same ideals of federal government aid and assistance that was never enumerated in our historical and principled governing document.

"Yet Hayes quickly learned that Republicans disagreed about what those deficiencies were. Californians wanted him to take a tougher stance against Chinese immigration." (By One Vote: The Disputed Presidential Election of 1876, The Campaign, Michael F. Holt, University of Press Kansas, 2008, page 121).

If the federal government would have never had taken such a drastic stance against any sort of immigration of any peoples. Then we would not have suffered the troubles of todays with the constant meddling of the general government into the naturalization clause.

We all see that California, which should have the beacon of a new light to the other sovereign States was instead a tragic sense to the rules of federalism. It appears that California has had (and still does) a very dependent congressional delegation, always putting their selfish needs of their state first and against the needs of the Constitution. The sad thing is that there are other congressional delegations alike seeking the same dependent aid. I guess with the shattered states in the south, the new dependent states are out west. It is something that Henry Clay did not want to create as he campaigned this same issue in his 1824 fight for the presidency.

It is California's problem to deal with any immigration situation affecting their state. It does not need to involve the General Government of the United States. How can we explain it to the demagogue respondents of the federal government to let the SOVEREIGN states enforce the naturalization clause of the Constitution without affecting the public coffers of other states?

If the federal government's high court would have let the states enforce this clause back before the civil war. We would have seen a true federalism republic of union of sovereign states. With arrogance comes ignorance as that is what we see in our present status of this American union.

"Still others, including John Sherman, cited the importance of exploiting anti-Catholic sentiment and urged Hayes to affirm his commitment to a constitutional amendment on the schools question, especially since the Democratic platform appeared to oppose one by pronouncing public education exclusively a state affair." (By One Vote: The Disputed Presidential Election of 1876, A Pivotal Congressional Session, Michael F. Holt, University of Press Kansas, 2008, page 121).

John Sherman, a political statesman from Ohio. Also, a member of the Sherman Family, including brother to union general William T. Sherman, the butcher of Atlanta. I see authoritarianism runs within that family.

This nation has had lots of anti-sentiment feelings and emotions in just about anything. It is quite alright to have those feelings and ways to express them in a healthy and peaceful matter. It is in the First Amendment to our federal Constitution.

"Congress shall make no law or abridging the freedom of speech, or of the press; or the right of the people peaceably to assemble..."

This right is to be considered in the public settings and environment. In the private world, if they do not receive public funds, then the first amendment does not apply for this guaranteed right.

What I do not agree is that they show these feelings in a violent fashion and including involving actions patronaged by the federal government.

When I see this individual from Ohio, sibling to one of the butchers of the union army, petitioned a presidential candidate to support an anti-Catholic measure for a federal constitutional amendment is blatantly tyrannical and autocratic.

It has been eleven years since we fought a bloody conflict over race equality. Was John Sherman prepared to launch this nation into another conflict based over a religious holy civil war?

If you believe this nation was founded on Judeo-Christian values, then you are sadly mistaken. This nation was founded, ratified, and affirmed to be a nation of non-religious affiliations by any government: federal or state.

This is another reason why I despise the political party system, especially this two-political party system.

A two-party system switches on platform like daily underwear change. One day, the Republican Party is for a federal-government-mandated education system, and then later they are against it. The same goes for the Democratic Party. They both want control but at their own power and discretion.

Prior to 1824, we knew where which entity stood for the appropriate policy. On federal policies, it was known that diplomacy, treasury, and war-like policies were the policies of the General Government. On the rest, commerce, education, the common welfare belongs to each of the sovereign States. But 1824 changed everything and hence it made a huge dent in the rules of federalism. Now we see where the people wanted and still want the General Government of the United States to dictate these national directives onto the states. And not having any concern or regard to the Constitution or the rules of federalism.

* * *

Government civil service has always been a problem since 1800, when the exiting president, President John Adams issued an order to grant a civil service post to William Marbury. Then later that post was rightfully revoked by the entering Secretary of State James Madison. But unfortunately, rescinded by an arrogant federal high court and its high Magistrate John Marshall.

For ever more, the theory of judicial review has plagued this nation for central government control for whatever issue has come up the high court. Now judicial review has plagued our electoral clauses at present times. Government civil service should be applied by merit alone, not by spoils or privilege.

"The spoils system and especially congressmen's control over executive appointments, Hayes maintained, had destroyed the ideal of independent government service envisioned by the founders. Because congressmen and senators now allotted federal offices in their districts and states, "the offices in these cases have become not merely rewards for party service, but rewards for services for party leaders. This system destroys the independence of the separate departments of the Government. It tends directly to extravagance and official incapacity. It is a temptation to dishonesty." (By One Vote: The Disputed Presidential Election of 1876, The Campaign, Michael F. Holt, University of Press Kansas, 2008, page 123).

I have doubt of Hayes' campaign and quite frankly his statement regarding the civil service that has led into an unprecedented and unconstitutional wave of civil service precedents. This union's national government was established to have their branches of powers separated and separated among themselves. That is how you maintain a sense of honesty and integrity within the government.

Hayes, the Republican candidate for president in 1876 has been corrupted by this system that the framers did not create. They envisioned a civil service system of non-partisanships and political bargains. But sadly, President Adams concocted at the last hours of his term to create a dismay for the incoming administration.

This civil service system was never meant to reward party service or to reward party leaders. It was to reward the merit of the officer. Also, to protect the integrity and respect of the Constitution.

It is the duty of the national Congress' job to keep everyone honest from the executive branch to themselves. An honest Congress approves of an honest man, there is no foul stench of partisanship or corruption. But a dishonest Congress approves of a dishonest man, dishonesty flourishes through the halls of government, both federal and state.

"The founders "neither expected nor desired from the public servant any partisan service"; rather, they intended that civil servants should be secure in their tenure except for malfeasance or incapacity. "If elected, I shall conduct the administration of the Government upon these principles, and all constitutional powers vested in the Executive will be employed to establish this reform." (By One Vote: The Disputed Presidential Election of 1876, The Campaign, Michael F. Holt, University of Press Kansas, 2008, page 123-124).

This is the presidential candidate's lie to the American electorate. This has been the same lie in 1824 to this election and to the present. Ever since, the first election that was not a constitutional framer nominated for the executive branch, the political point of view has changed. The candidates always made this claim, that they will not behave in an irrational manner and behavior and always to their constitutional framers' principles. While the first thing they do is behave the opposite and install tyrannical unconstitutional policies.

* * *

"Whatever his professions, Democrats charged, Hayes would be a prisoner of "Grantism" if elected." (By One Vote: The Disputed Presidential Election of 1876, The Campaign, Michael F. Holt, University of Press Kansas, 2008, page 125).

I could say the same thing of Samuel Tilden, would he be a prisoner of Jeff Davis, if elected.

How about our candidates be beacons of the Framers, rather than prisoners of a party or cult? I blame the very idea of populism and vanity that has been installed in every single election since 1824.

This has always been the same and truthful sentiment of many American electorates that a candidate's views and positions will be influenced and compromised by a former statesman or statesmen. Ever since the 1824 election, many candidates steered away from the constitutional framers' principles and approached to other ideals and vile principles.

Even before the 1876 election, the federal government and certain dependent individuals wanted to control the state elections for their own benefit, and not for the benefit for the state sovereign doctrine. Every time the national government intervened in state's actions, they create chaos and dismay.

"In 1872 Congress passed a law to standardize congressional elections. Starting in 1876 all elections for members of the House of Representatives were to be held on the Tuesday after the first Monday in November of even-numbered years." (By One Vote: The Disputed Presidential Election of 1876, The Elections of 1876, Michael F. Holt, University of Press Kansas, 2008, page 152).

"In 1875, however, Congress had revised that law to exempt states that would be forced to amend their state constitutions to reschedule state and congressional elections for November. In 1876 this revision meant that in addition to Alabama's gubernatorial election in August, the Republican strongholds of Vermont and Maine would select governors and congressmen in September, as would Georgia on October 4. The new state of Colorado, along with Indiana, Ohio, and West Virginia, would elect state officials and congressmen on October 10, four weeks before the balloting for president." (By One Vote: The Disputed Presidential Election of 1876, The Elections of 1876, Michael F. Holt, University of Press Kansas, 2008, page 152-153).

Yes, Congress has the power to select the dates for the national congressional representation elections in Washington as stated in Article IV. But Congress must be careful not to step over the state sovereignty's doctrine on the electoral clauses.

Even the republican strong-hold states were filled with deep vulnerability to be switched overdue in part of these electoral acts passed by Congress.

"No one expected Republicans to carry Alabama or Georgia." (By One Vote: The Disputed Presidential Election of 1876, The Elections of 1876, Michael F. Holt, University of Press Kansas, 2008, page 153).

And no one expects the Democrats to carry Pennsylvania or Massachusetts. States in where the majority party holds the most legislative seats, is probably the winner of those presidential electoral votes.

There were three highly contested states in the 1876 presidential election. These were three states with a republican-controlled state legislature. These states were Florida, South Carolina, and Louisiana. In 2000, it always came down to Florida, but in 1876, it came down to three.

"In Florida, the only state of the three where blacks did not constitute a majority of the registered electorate, Republicans renominated incumbent carpetbag Governor Marcellus Stearns. Stearns was the bitter enemy of Republican Senator Simon Conover, who briefly ran as an Independent to prevent Stearns reelection. That republican split gave the edge to Democrat George F. Drew, a former Whig and opponent of secession who might appeal to moderate whites." (By One Vote: The Disputed Presidential Election of 1876, The Elections of 1876, Michael F. Holt, University of Press Kansas, 2008, page 163).

Florida has always been a mixed bag of political nuts. Even though, Florida had a strong republican controlled legislature during Reconstruction, it created a haven of a mixed bag of political nuts.

The state of Florida was the third state to join the confederacy, right after Mississippi. To have a progressive Democrat, from New Hampshire, to always have been in opposition to secession to curb moderate Floridians on that election. It is stating that Florida will go wherever the sunny sunshine winds will blow.

"In South Carolina, incumbent Republican Governor Daniel H. Chamberlain was seeking reelection. He had pleased white taxpayers and alienated many black Republicans by slashing expenditures and state tax rates after his election of 1874. For a while, therefore, grateful Democrats considered letting Chamberlain run unopposed. Instead, they nominated Civil War Wade Hampton, perhaps the best known and most popular white man in the state. Hampton, not Tilden, was expected to generate a huge increase in white turnout." (By One Vote: The Disputed Presidential Election of 1876, The Elections of 1876, Michael F. Holt, University of Press Kansas, 2008, page 164).

Even though, the state legislature of South Carolina was Republican since the beginning of Reconstruction, the vast majority thinking of the population and its former state officials have always been with the hearts of a Democrat.

This is the first state that declared secession. Also, let us not forget that it was the first state to act as an aggressor towards this American republic with the bombardment of the federal army fort, Ft. Sumpter. This state was going to be a highly contested state for the presidency of the 1876 elections.

"In these three states, as well as elsewhere in the South, the basic Democratic message was the same: white supremacy required ousting Republicans from control of state-governments or preventing them from retaking it where Democrats were already in the saddle." (By One Vote: The Disputed Presidential Election of 1876, The Elections of 1876, Michael F. Holt, University of Press Kansas, 2008, page 164).

"On November 7, 1876, some 2 million more men cast presidential ballots than had done so four years earlier. Hundreds of thousands of Republicans and even more Democrats had sat out the 1872 election. Nonetheless, it is obvious that both parties also mobilized new supporters. As noted earlier, the turnout rate of eligible voters soared from 71.3 percent in 1872 to 81.1 percent in 1876." (By One Vote: The Disputed Presidential Election of 1876, The Elections of 1876, Michael F. Holt, University of Press Kansas, 2008, page 165).

"The distribution of popular votes among the states, not the size of the nationwide plurality, was what counted, of course, and those votes (excluding the Prohibitionist votes in 1872 and 1876) are recorded in table 5. Table 6, in turn, lists the turnout rates by state in 1872 and 1876, as well as the size of the Democratic and Republican margin of victory over the other and the victorious party's percentage of the total vote in each state." (By One Vote: The Disputed Presidential Election of 1876, The Elections of 1876, Michael F. Holt, University of Press Kansas, 2008, page 165-166).

Voter turnout typically does come at the general presidential re-election of the incumbent president. But why is everywhere I read, from the election to 1824 to 1876, to 2000, to 2016 and 2020 elections that we focus on the infamy popular vote? When will people finally realize that this vote is meaningless in a presidential general election. We must be focusing more on the electoral college vote than this one.

Political parties may increase their popular support, but in the end, it is what political party holds the majority in the state legislature to give the win for the presidency of the American republic of sovereign States.

Yet again, here is an author discussing an important presidential general election affecting the entire sovereign States. He brings out the infamous popular vote that have dragged elections after elections filled with anxiety and frustration.

After a heavily contested election, now comes the counting of electoral votes and the less constitutional importance on counting of popular votes.

"Rutherford Hayes, for one, remained convinced for almost a week that he had lost the election." (By One Vote: The Disputed Presidential Election of 1876, The Disputed Results, Michael F. Holt, University of Press Kansas, 2008, page 175).

"Later in the same diary entry, Hayes expressed a belief that became firmer with each passing day: "A fair day election in the South would undoubtedly have given us a large majority of the electoral votes, and a decided preponderance of the popular vote." Yet later that same day he received a telegram from William Dennison (Ohio's wartime governor) in Washington "which seems to open it all up again." "You are undoubtedly elected next President of the US.," wrote Dennison." "Desperate attempts are being made to defeat you in Louisiana, South Carolina, & Florida but they will not succeed." (By One Vote: The Disputed Presidential Election of 1876, The Disputed Results, Michael F. Holt, University of Press Kansas, 2008, page 175).

By One (1) Constitutional Vote in 1876: The three highly contested sovereign States:

Florida – 4 electoral votes	Republican controlled state legislature – Hayes victory
Louisiana – 8 electoral votes	Republican controlled state legislature – Hayes victory
South Carolina – 7 electoral votes	Republican controlled state legislature – Hayes victory

"No doubt both fraud and violence intervened to produce the results." (By One Vote: The Disputed Presidential Election of 1876, The Disputed Results, Michael F. Holt, University of Press Kansas, 2008, page 175).

Violence intervened itself in such a crucial election on account of the claims of fraud. Claims of fraud that there was never any truthful account to it.

"A threat against our American electoral college is a threat to liberty that established this nation." Anybody who calls our American electoral college, a fraud, they are still American, but their credibility sunk to a new low.

This election came just after four months, this celebrated its 100th's birthday of independence. And yet, there were individuals seeking to split this nation apart if they do not get the electoral results they wanted.

Because of the unconstitutionality of others, the rest of the nation had to endure new procedures that do not coincide with the Constitution.

"On the session's opening day, Abram Hewitt introduced a resolution that the House send committees to Florida, Louisiana, and South Carolina to expose the fraudulent findings of the Republican returning boards." (By One Vote: The Disputed Presidential Election of 1876, The Disputed Resolved, Michael F. Holt, University of Press Kansas, 2008, page 204).

This was the ultimate dread to our American republic when partisan politics takes over principled politics. Why is a congressman from one political party started to investigate state legislatures controlled by another political party? If that is the case, then why was there not an investigation of state legislatures controlled by the same political party that the honorable member Mr. Hewitt was partisan of it. If they were talking about popular vote disfranchisements among the several states, then yes, investigations should have been demanded to the several states like Mississippi, Alabama, and Georgia.

"As one of the Republicans who had gone to Florida protested, Democrats had refused to let them see anything." (By One Vote: The Disputed Presidential Election of 1876, The Disputed Resolved, Michael F. Holt, University of Press Kansas, 2008, page 205).

"South Carolina was a special case. Even the Democrats on the investigating committee announced that Hayes had clearly carried it. Therefore, the case for Democrats would make about South Carolina was not that Tilden deserved its votes, but that Hayes did not deserve them either, because the intimidating presence of federal marshals and troops had prevented of both blacks and whites from voting for Tilden. Voiding South Carolina votes, not delivering them for Tilden, would be their strategy." (By One Vote: The Disputed Presidential Election of 1876, The Disputed Resolved, Michael F. Holt, University of Press Kansas, 2008, page 205).

If Democrats from up north were on a crusade to instigate fraud claims, while Democrats from the south were denying showing any fraud inquiry. Then who were the fraudsters of this election?

Federal marshals and union army presence were only in the former rebellious states because of certain individuals that were violating newly added constitutional amendments after a bloody civil war. Their presence had nothing to do with the election. To concoct this idea that federal law enforcement and military presence were preventing blacks from voting for Tilden, a Democrat, is an idea with no factual evidence. It does not give any factual evidence to promote this idea of electoral fraud.

"Democratic confidence in that scenario grew when Congressman Abram Hewitt still Chairman of the Democratic National Committee, secured an interview with Grant at the White House on December 3 and then infuriated the president by announcing that Grant believed the House should throw out Louisiana's electoral votes." (By One Vote: The Disputed Presidential Election of 1876, The Disputed Resolved, Michael F. Holt, University of Press Kansas, 2008, page 206).

"The language of the Twelfth Amendment to the Constitution was at once crystal clear and maddeningly vague about this point. It specified that on the day when representatives and senators assembled to hear the counting of electoral votes, "the President of the Senate shall, in the presence of the Senate and the House of Representatives, open all the certificates and the votes shall then be counted." But by whom?" (By

One Vote: The Disputed Presidential Election of 1876, The Disputed Resolved, Michael F. Holt, University of Press Kansas, 2008, page 207).

Again, any hint of partisanship in the halls of government shall be dismissed immediately.

The Twelfth Amendment was established after the 1800 election, for a couple of reasons. Instead of the runner-up presidential candidate becomes the vice-president elect. The presidential candidate chooses a person to be his running mate, the vice-president and from a different sovereign state of residency. But also, the vice-presidential official duties remained to be the Senate President. One of its duties is to be the tiebreaker of a vote in the national Senate.

As the electoral votes are collected and official-ized by their respective state legislature. They are sent to the national Congress for a final verifica-tion and call for the winner of the election. This is how elections are won, at least in this country, and respected by all.

"States alone, they maintained, had the exclusive power to appoint presidential electors. Once they were chosen, Congress had absolutely no constitu-tional power to dispute, challenge, or change what the states had done. To make such an attempt was a fragrant violation of states' rights and an uncon-scionable consolidation of power in Congress at the expense of those rights." (By One Vote: The Disputed Presidential Election of 1876, The Disputed Resolved, Michael F. Holt, University of Press Kansas, 2008, page 211).

This is not the first attack from the General Government of the United States on the state sovereign doctrine, and it will not be the last. But the federal government ignores the will of the States, let alone the will of the individual citizen.

The respective state legislators of each sovereign State have spoken in this 1876 election. Florida, Louisiana, and South Carolina, with a solid political party in control have given their electoral votes to the presidential candidacy of Rutherford B. Hayes.

Those willing to distort the will of the sovereign State, as prescribed in their Article I and II electoral powers and guaranteed in their Tenth Amendment right are distorting liberty. Whether it be somebody from the national government, or a plebe mob, it is wrong and unconstitutional.

"From the start, both committees agreed that members of the Supreme Court should serve on the tribunal, and the Republican *New York Times*, for one, considered this judicial participation outrageous." (By One Vote: The Disputed Presidential Election of 1876, The Disputed Resolved, Michael F. Holt, University of Press Kansas, 2008, page 212).

For Congress to agree and suggest an electoral tribunal or electoral commission and to include members of the high court goes against the separation of powers of the federal government.

The Chief Justice of the Supreme Court is the magistrate of a presidential conviction trial, but he serves as an impartial entity. What Congress is suggesting is having the third branch of the national government act as a voting entity in *chusing* the next president of these United States.

I understand that the forty-fourth Congress from 1875 to 1877, the Congress that saw and managed the 1876 elections was a divided Congress. The House of Representatives was Democrat controlled. The Senate was Republican controlled. I can see why members of the Republican party wanted to entail this scheme to establish commission and bring in a republican-nominated court into deciding an election. Which is clearly the official duty of the Congress and Congress alone.

If there is an electoral vote deadlock or electoral vote dispute. Then the election heads to the national House of Representatives for deliberation and vote. To involve this commission and members of the high court, I would call it unconstitutional and no need for this tribalism politics.

This 1876 electoral commission was made up fifteen members. Five members from each House and Senate and five members of the Supreme Court. In the end, these unelected individuals of a commission voted to decide to give the presidency to Rutherford B. Hayes. The national government likes to put on an amateur theatrical show to produce no credible or constitutional results. The only thing they will show result is more chaos and dismay towards a more troubled republic.

If all members of our national Congress accepted these electoral vote results, then we would not have seen this unconstitutional debacle. The plebs of this American republic would not have the urge to show force against not against the government but at the Constitution.

"Such disagreement was inevitable "in every instance where matters of dispute are made the subject of arbitration under the forms of law." (By One Vote: The Disputed Presidential Election of 1876, The Disputed Resolved, Michael F. Holt, University of Press Kansas, 2008, page 2241-242).

This country will always have disagreements because it is in the human's imperfect of their character. With those common disagreements to have, peaceably sentiments must we have to have these joint dissimilarities. I only disagree with how this election was decided. It was left by the bureaucratic and legislative train wreck of the national government. It was not left to the will of the sovereign State and their legislatures in these three states. If all respected the will of the state legislature efforts of these three states to choose their state electors. These state electors chose the best candidate to fit the presidency of these United States. Then we would not have sought to obtain the advice of the federal government. Or the advice of a federal electoral commission mixed in with various members of the national government. This is not the American Constitution way to seek a presidential electoral closure.

Ironic, in 1876, it was three states that had an electoral dispute: Florida, Louisiana, and South Carolina. In 2000, it was one state: Florida. In 2020, it was again three, Pennsylvania, Wisconsin, and Georgia. In the end, it is the ignorance of a few Americans that will never understand the will of the Constitution and its sovereign State doctrine that have these wins for these states.

"Most Democrats never accepted such a rosy conclusion. Throughout Hayes's presidency, they insisted
that it was illegitimate." (By One Vote: The Disputed Presidential
Election of 1876, The Disputed Resolved, Michael F. Holt, University of Press
Kansas, 2008, page 242).

"If the Democratic House have been foolishly
'fleeced' by a Republican 'confidence game,'" a
Vermont Democrat wrote to Tilden on February 20,
"neither you nor the Democratic Party behind you are
bound by fraud." (By One Vote: The Disputed Presidential Election of
1876, The Disputed Resolved, Michael F. Holt, University of Press Kansas, 2008,
page 242).

"Although many Democrats had earlier complained
of Tilden's seeming passivity during the struggle,
they now, at the last moment, called on him to lead
the party in resistance to the commission's decisions.
"It is your duty to call upon your party immediately to
inaugurate you, and they will swarm from every section of the country to carry out your wishes," vowed
a Chicago Democrat on February 21. "They await
only a reason, and a leader, to rise up in arms." "I
would never submit to the damnable fraud," echoed
a Rochester, New York, supporter three days later. "I
would advise friends to resist to the last extremity &
until eternal justice prevails." "Counsel resistance.
We dare not submit to fraud," New Jersey's James M.
Scovel telegraphed from Philadelphia on February
26." (By One Vote: The Disputed Presidential Election of 1876, The Disputed
Resolved, Michael F. Holt, University of Press Kansas, 2008, page 242-243).

"We think it is your imperative duty to contest the
title of the Presidency, before the Supreme Court,"

urged a Pennsylvanian in February." (By One Vote: The Disputed Presidential Election of 1876, The Disputed Resolved, Michael F. Holt, University of Press Kansas, 2008, page 243).

By reading all these comments in against the electoral winner of the 1876 presidential election. It does remind me of the same comments made in 2000, and upcoming in 2024. Not as much as 1824, I guess because even the first Framers' heirs knew the constitutional process and the will of the sovereign State's doctrine.

People are quite eager to submit to an electoral vote fraud with no basis of truthful of evidence. A New Jersey man told the Democratic presidential nominee that 'he dare not submit to fraud'. It is very valid to spew words of discontent, but not valid to spew words of alleged fraud charges.

"We think it is your imperative duty to contest the title of the Presidency, before the Supreme Court," urged a Pennsylvanian in February."

"Cruz, who has argued nine cases before the Supreme Court, tweeted Monday that he stood "ready to present the oral argument" in a case from Pennsylvania Republicans urging the court to block certification of the commonwealth's election results." (Trump asked Ted Cruz to argue Texas election lawsuit if it reaches Supreme Court, by Betsy Klein, Jim Acosta, and Caroline Kennedy, CNN, Wed., December 09, 2020).

If I do not agree of members of the Supreme Court being part of this 1876 commission. I do not agree involving the Supreme Court to dispute the will of a sovereign State's electoral votes. If I also did not agree how the Supreme Court handled the 2000 election. The Supreme Court is truly not to decide electoral disputes, as it is not dictated in the Constitution.

It was not right in 1876, in 2000, and in 2020 to involve the Supreme Court. It is not right in the future to further involve the high court. It is high time, we learned our lesson and know our Constitution will not allow it!

On December 11, 2020, the high court decided that "Texas lacks Article III standing to sue other states over how they conduct their own elections. Case dismissed. It was a *Per Curiam* decision, a statement decision made by Associate Justice Samuel Alito, joined by Associate Justice Clarence Thomas. As many people may not agree with my statements regarding this high court. But this court remains to be the most unpredictable court in all United States legal and political history.

"My dear Sir, enter suite at once against Rutherford B. Hayes in the name and in behalf of the People of the United States forbidding him the exercise of that office and keep him in court the whole of the next four years and you will save your country." This Democratic soldier advised his punitive commander to be in Washington on inauguration day so that Tilden could personally "serve the writ on him [Hayes], if he takes the oath. Serve the moment afterward before he makes his [inaugural] speech." Now that would have been a scene for the history books." (By One Vote: The Disputed Presidential Election of 1876, The Disputed Resolved, Michael F. Holt, University of Press Kansas, 2008, page 243).

This is quite an interesting quote from an American that is quite subjective to not knowing its own Constitution. The ignorance of a few commits the stupidity of the masses. As we have seen the masses commit acts of treason in 2020 to 2021. We have had share of this same sentiment back in 1876 and quite closely in 1824.

We, as Americans will never advance to true constitutional scholars, if we decide to think like mad men, rather than intellectual constitutional men. We, as Americans need to move forward not with violent sentiment but with principle sentiment. With the true wordings of the Constitutional Framers as we move forward. But, unfortunately, in the next chapters, we have a long road ahead. A long road ahead to achieve the sane constitutionality of elections guaranteed by our framers and instituted by our current and past individuals of government.

2000 Election and 2020 Election

Article I, Section IV, Clause I

"The Times, Places and Manner of holding Elections for Senators and Representatives, shall be prescribed in each State by the Legislature thereof; but the Congress may at any time by Law make or alter such Regulations, except as to the Places of chusing [sic] Senators.

Article II, Section I, Clause II

"Each State shall appoint, in such Manner as the Legislature thereof may direct, a Number of Electors, equal to the whole Number of Senators and Representatives to which the State may be entitled in the Congress: but no Senator or Representative, or Person holding an Office of Trust or Profit under the United States, shall be appointed an Elector.

These sovereign United States of America are the last form of representative republic. These sovereign United States of America are not a united democracy. There is a reason behind this type of representative republic form of government. These states are formed as "a more perfect union." These sovereign states are the driving force behind every aspect of the rules of federalism and the Constitution.

It is the states' job to enforce the electoral law, not the federal government.

When the sovereign states lost their representation in the national Congress with the passage of the Seventeenth Amendment, it was a huge blow to the rules of federalism. And if we lose the Electoral College, then we will no longer submit to the rules of federalism, only the rules of tyranny.

The progressive movement started with Theodore Roosevelt and Robert LaFollete. Then Woodrow Wilson took it over with his Wilsonian Progressive ideologies and attacks on our rules of federalism. These are the first Americans to disavow our republic's rules by imposing totalitarian, contradictory and unconstitutional policies onto the states.

We have begun to go under this path of destruction to our republic. If these progressives continue like this, it will be the final death blow to our American republic of sovereign States. We cannot let these progressives, whether called Wilsonian Progressives or FDR liberals, New Democrats or even a newer group, New Trump Republicans, install totalitarian rules against the rules of federalism.

If true believers of our federalism rules are not careful, we may also lose our beloved Electoral College, which is our last form of republic representation. The Electoral College is the correct way of electing the chief executive of the nation. Where the fifty sovereign states are telling the federal government, "We are in control."

We cannot let the federal government, and especially the high court, dictate every single policy onto the states. And this includes elections. That was never the intention of the constitutional framers. The prime intention was to preserve the rules of federalism and that power belongs to the states! I truly cannot stress enough in this article that, "power belongs to the sovereign states, and not the federal government."

When I read the following ruling of *Bush v. Gore*, 2000; and the 2020 election debacle, and soon to be the 2024 election chaos, the rules of federalism must apply. These rulings showed to the American citizenry that there is such a thing called the rules of federalism and a state sovereign doctrine. That is what I have been advocating all this time. I will never accede to federal autocracy. My loyalty is to the Constitution and the rules of federalism that bind this republic together.

The November 7, 2000, election began no different than any other in election history. The voters, popular and electors, in all fifty sovereign states went to the polls to cast their ballot for their local, state, and national representatives in government, including for president.

Then came Palm Beach County, Florida, where the voters were not aligning their voting ballot properly and not following the proper voting standard as stated by Florida electoral law. This law was passed by the state legislature.

Then Metro-Dade, Broward and Volusia Counties came forward and started to complain that the ballots were not being penetrated and leaving dimple chad or hanging chad.

According to the state of Florida electoral law, an actual penetration of the ballot is constituted as a legal ballot. That is the law of the sovereign State of Florida and no other state has the right to interject their standards of voting onto the disputed state's election.

We are going to review together the concurring opinion by the Chief Justice William Rehnquist to see if there was a violation of the equal protection clause. The concurring opinion agrees with the *Per Curiam* opinion. We will also see if there was irreparable harm toward the petitioner George W. Bush in this election. We will also review the dissenting opinions Justices Stevens, and Ginsburg to see how they feel about the electoral process in our American federalism republic.

"In most cases, comity and respect for federalism compel us to defer to the decisions of state courts on issues of state law. That practice reflects our understanding that the decisions of state courts are definitive pronouncements of the will of the States as sovereigns." (Concurring Opinion on Bush v. Gore by Chief Justice William Rehnquist, 2000).

It claims that each state is not only sovereign but independent. And with independence comes self-reliance and responsibility.

It appears that in this ruling and other judgments that the high court has established a precedent on electoral disputes on Article II, Section I, Clause II on the election of an elector. We truly cannot let the federal government and other sovereign state entities dictate a directive to the state in question. It claims that each state is not only sovereign but independent, but that with independence comes self-reliance and responsibility.

"Of course, in ordinary cases, the distribution of powers among the branches of a State's government raises no questions of federal constitutional law, subject to the requirement that the government be republican in character. See U.S. Const., Article IV, Section 4. But there are a few exceptional cases in which the Constitution imposes a duty or confers a particular branch of a State's government. This is one of them. Article II, Section I, Clause II, provides that "[e]ach State shall appoint, in such a Manner as the Legislature thereof may direct," electors for President and Vice-President. (Emphasis added). Thus, ***113** the text of the election law itself, and not just its interpretation by the courts of the States, takes on independent significance." (Concurring Opinion on Bush v. Gore by Chief Justice William Rehnquist, 2000).

The Supreme Court states that we as a republic must respect all branches of government—federal and individual, independent states. With separated powers, comes individual responsibility of each power. Any attempt to grab the power of another must be stopped by one of the other branches to return to a stable separated power.

"In any election but a Presidential election, the Florida Supreme Court can give as little or as much deference to Florida's executives as it chooses, so far as Article II is concerned, and this Court will have no cause to question the Court's actions. But, with respect to a Presidential election, the court must be mindful of the legislature's role under Article II in choosing the manner of appointing electors and deferential to those *****535** bodies expressly empowered by the legislature to carry out its constitutional mandate." (Concurring Opinion on Bush v. Gore by Chief Justice William Rehnquist, 2000).

This statement made by the late Chief Justice William Rehnquist speaks to all the sovereign state legislatures in this American republic. The Supreme Court of each sovereign state has no jurisdiction, let alone constitutional jurisdiction on presidential elections.

If people would really read Supreme Court briefs, or the Constitution, they would realize how our republic has been formed and created. If President Trump would have directed his legal team to lobby the legislature of those affected states to change the law. We would not have dragged another election through the courts. A court- dragging by Trump himself makes it even more of an unconstitutional figure and indeed tainted his presidential legacy.

"In order to determine whether a state court has infringed upon the legislature's authority, we necessarily must examine the law of the State as it existed prior to the action of the court. Though we generally defer to state courts on the interpretation of state law—see, e.g., Mullaney v. Wilbur, 421 U.S. 684, 95 S. Ct. 1881, 44 L.Ed.2d 508 (1975)—there are of course areas in which the Constitution requires this Court to undertake an independent, if still deferential, analysis of state law."

(Concurring Opinion on Bush v. Gore by Chief Justice William Rehnquist, 2000).

The Supreme Court in this decision stated that the interference of the judicial system in a presidential election would only count once. People must realize that we cannot use the judicial process as their own personal lawyer. There is a process to argue your grievances to the government. Also you cannot skip or use different branches of government to petition that grievance.

"The inquiry does not imply a disrespect for *state courts* but rather a respect for the constitutionally prescribed role of *state legislatures*. To attach definitive weight to the pronouncement of a state court, when the very question at issue is whether the court has actually departed from the statutory meaning, would be abdicate our responsibility to enforce the explicit requirements of Article II." (Concurring Opinion on Bush v. Gore by Chief Justice William Rehnquist, 2000).

As I wrote earlier, there are procedures in place for the government to conduct business regarding your grievances. A citizen cannot decide to skip certain steps to get the justice that they desire. If that citizen does, then everybody is entitled to do the same and that is not fair. Speaking of fairness, the government must serve as the primary fairness entity. The government, whether the executive, legislative or judicial, federal, or state branches, must provide to all citizens equal treatment under law.

"Acting pursuant to its constitutional grant of authority, the Florida Legislature has created a detailed, if not perfectly crafted, statutory

For a court to take on the role of the state legislature would be just as tyrannical as for the chief executive to take on the role of a state legislature.

scheme that provides for appointment of Presidential electors by direct election... The Legislature ***536 has designated the Secretary as their "Chief election officer," with the responsibility to "[o]btain and maintain uniformity in the application, operation, and interpretation of the election laws." (Concurring Opinion on Bush v. Gore by Chief Justice William Rehnquist, 2000).

It is the sovereign state's own legislative power that grants electoral laws. It is stated in the federal Constitution, to fully be interpreted to the letter, that the states choose their electors in their own manner and set their own voting standards. For a court to take on the role of the state legislature would be just as tyrannical as for the chief executive to take on the role of a state legislature.

"The state legislature has also provided mechanisms both for protesting election returns and for contesting certified *117 election results. Section 102.166 governs protests." (Concurring Opinion on Bush v. Gore by Chief Justice William Rehnquist, 2000).

"In its first decision, *Palm Beach Canvassing Bd., v. Harris*, 772 S. 2d. 1220 (2000) (*Harris I*), the Florida Supreme Court extended the 7-day statutory certification deadline established *118 by the legislature. This modification of the code, by lengthening the protest period, necessarily shortened the contest period for Presidential elections. Underlying the extension of the certification deadline **537 was a matter of significance: The certified winner would enjoy presumptive validity, making a contest proceeding by the losing candidate an uphill battle. In its latest opinion, however, the court empties certifi-cation of virtually all legal consequence during the contest, and in doing so departs from the provisions enacted by the Florida Legislature." (Concurring Opinion on Bush v. Gore by Chief Justice William Rehnquist, 2000).

"Moreover, the court's interpretation of "legal vote," and hence its decision to order a contest-period recount, plainly departed from the legislative scheme. Florida statutory law cannot reasonably be thought to require the counting of improperly *119 marked bal-lots. Each Florida precinct before election day pro-vides instructions on how properly to cast a vote, Fla. Stat. Ann. Section 101.46 (1992); each polling place on election day contains a working model of the vot-ing machine it uses, Fla. Stat. Ann. Section 101.5611 (Supp.2001); and each voting booth contains a sam-ple ballot, Section 101.46. In precincts using a punch-card ballots, voters are instructed to punch out the ballot clearly." (Concurring Opinion on Bush v. Gore by Chief Justice William Rehnquist, 2000).

The only entity to define the legality of a vote is not set by its own court but by its own state legislature. In 1992, the state legislature and the late Gov. Lawton Chiles set the voting standards of Florida elections for president and vice president. For the Florida court to take the power to define a legal vote is just how rogue and arrogant the federal government behaves when it takes power away from the sovereign states.

The Florida voting standard in 2000 is as clear as the Pennsylvania voting standard in 2020. As we saw in the Keystone State. Their own state court did not alter or change their own laws to satisfy the petitioner, Donald J. Trump. In 2020, that state legislature saw fit to introduce an electoral law of vote-by-mail. Let us remember that it was an Executive Order, signed by then-President Trump to allow states to pass voter-by-mail electoral law standards.

"But as we indicated in our remand of the earlier case, in a Presidential election the clearly expressed intent of the legislature must prevail. And there is no basis for reading the Florida statutes as requiring the counting of improperly marked ballots, as an examination of the Florida Supreme Court's textual analysis shows. We will not parse that analysis here, except to note that the principal provision of the Election Code on which it relied, Section 101.5614(5), was, as Chief Justice Wells pointed out in his dissent in *Gore v. Harris*, 772 So.2d 1243, 1267 (2000) (*Harris II*), entirely irrelevant. The State's Attorney General (who was supporting the Gore challenge) confirmed in oral argument here that never before the present election had a manual recount been conducted on the basis of the contention that "undervotes" should have been examined to determine voter intent. Tr. Of Oral Arg. In Bush v. Palm Beach County Canvassing Bd., O.T. 2000, No. 00-836, pp. 39-40, 2000 WL 1763666, at *39-*40; cf. Broward County Canvassing Board v. Hogan, 607 So.2d 508, 509 (Fla.Ct.App.1992) (denial of recount for failure to count ballots with "hanging paper chads"). For the court to step away from the established practice, prescribed by the Secretary, the state official charged by the legislature with "responsibility to… [o]btain and maintain uniformity in the application, operation and interpretation of the election laws," Section 97.012(1), was to depart from the legislative scheme." (Concurring Opinion on Bush v. Gore by Chief Justice William Rehnquist, 2000).

Each state is sovereign and autonomous from each other in creating their own laws —from elections to gun rights to family rights. Each sovereign state does not contradict the principled document that binds this republic together. The Constitution and to witness another sovereign state entity try to force their standards onto that affected state is beyond unconstitutional.

"The Constitution assigns to the States the primary responsibility for determining the manner of selecting the Presidential electors. See Art. II, Section 1, clause 2. When questions arise about the meaning of state laws, including election laws, it is our settled practice to accept the opinions of the highest courts of the States as providing the final answers. On rare occasions, however, either federal statutes or the federal Constitution may require federal judicial intervention in state elections. This is not such an occasion." (Dissenting Opinion on Bush v. Gore by Associate Justice John Paul Stevens, 2000).

"The legislative **540 power in Florida is subject to judicial review pursuant *124 to Article V of the Florida Constitution, and nothing in Article II of the Federal Constitution frees the state legislature from the constraints in the State Constitution that created it. Moreover, the Florida Legislature's own decision to employ a unitary code for all elections indicates that it intended the Florida Supreme Court to play the same role in Presidential elections that it has historically played in resolving electoral disputes. The Florida Supreme Court's exercise of appellate jurisdiction therefore was wholly consistent with, and indeed contemplated by, the grant of authority in Article II." (Dissenting Opinion on Bush v. Gore by Associate Justice John Paul Stevens, 2000).

It is not standard practice to accept any rulings that go against the rules of federalism. In the case of a state high court, there is a last resort for the rules of federalism to apply: The Supreme Court of the land. But within the states, whether the legislature, executive or courts, there is no power to contradict the Constitution.

This a one-time only occasion in where the high court of the land intervened for judicial review. It was due because the state court re-wrote the electoral law that contradicted with the current law set by the people's legislative assembly. The legislature is the only entity to change those codes per Article II of the Federal Constitution.

"*126 Admittedly, the use of differing sub-standards for determining voter intent in different counties employing similar voting systems may raise serious concerns. Those concerns are alleviated—if not eliminated—by the fact that a single impartial magistrate will ultimately adjudicate all objections arising from the recount process. Of course, as a general matter, "[t]he interpretation of constitutional principles must not be too literal. We must remember that the machinery of government would not work if it were allowed a little play in its joints." Bain Peanut Co. of Tex. V. Pinson, 282 U.S. 499, 501, 51 S. Ct. 228, 75 L.Ed. 482 (1931) (Holmes, J.). If it were otherwise, Florida's decision to leave each county the determination of what balloting system to employ—despite enormous differences in accuracy—might run afoul of equal protection. So, too, might the similar decisions of the vast majority of state legislatures to delegate to local authorities certain decisions with respect to voting systems and ballot design." (Dissenting Opinion on Bush v. Gore by Associate Justice John Paul Stevens, 2000).

"Florida law holds that all ballots that reveal intent of the voter constitute valid votes." (Dissenting Opinion on Bush v. Gore by Associate Justice John Paul Stevens, 2000).

The intent of the Florida voter is revealed when the ballot is penetrated. In reality, of course, is the true intent of the voter itself is when they have exercised their vote with accordance to the electoral laws and standards of therein state.

In Pennsylvania electoral law, the intent of the voter is revealed through a personal visit to the ballot box or a mail-in ballot. The Court recognized this electoral change and had to stand by it. The Pennsylvania state court saw fit not to alter the law as the Florida court did in 2000.

"Finally, neither in this case, nor in its earlier opinion in *Palm Beach County Canvassing Bd. V. Harris*, 772 So. 2d 1220 (2000), did the Florida Supreme Court make any substantive ***128** change in Florida electoral law. Its decisions were rooted in long-established precedent and were consistent with the relevant statutory provisions, taken as a whole. It did what courts do—it decided the case before it light of the legislature's intent to leave no legally cast vote uncounted. In doing so, it relied on the sufficiency of the general "intent of the voter" standard articulated by the state legislature, coupled with a procedure for ultimate review by an impartial judge, to resolve the concern about the disparate evaluations of contested ballots. If we assume—as I do—that the members of that court and the judges who would have carried out its mandate are impartial, its decision does not even raise a colorable federal question." (Dissenting Opinion on Bush v. Gore by Associate Justice John Paul Stevens, 2000).

If Justice Stevens believes this election did not raise a constitutional question, then I worry that future generations will seek to not trust our fellow members of this high court. The Florida Supreme Court did make a substantial change against the wishes of the Florida state legislature. They changed the voting standard and procedure in how to count ballots.

The Supreme Court chose wisely to respect the wishes of both the state legislatures of Florida and Pennsylvania. The rightful entities to alter or change the electoral procedure of their state as rightly put in Article II.

I respectfully dissent to Justice Stevens dissent. Because his dissent contradicts the Constitution and the matter of each sovereign states abilty to handle their election laws as they choose by the state legislature as granted by the federal Constitution.

"THE CHIEF JUSTICE acknowledges that provisions of Florida's Election Code "may well admit of more than interpretation." *Ante*, at 534 (concurring opinion). But instead of respecting the state high court's province to say what the State's Election Code means, THE CHIEF JUSTICE maintains that Florida's Supreme Court has veered so far from the ordinary practice of judicial review that what it did cannot ***136** properly be called judging. My colleagues have offered a reasonable construction of Florida's law. Their construction coincides with the view of one Florida's seven Supreme Court justices. *Gore v. Harris*, 772 So.2d 1273, 1291-1292 (Fla.2000) (on remand) (confirming, 6 to 1, the construction of Florida law advanced in *Gore*.)I might join THE CHIEF JUSTICE were it in my commission to interpret Florida law. But disagreement with the Florida's court interpretation of its own State's law does not warrant the conclusion that the justices of that court have legislated. There is no cause here to believe that the members of Florida's high court have done less than "their mortal best to discharge their oath of office," Sumner v. Mata, 449 U.S. 539, 549, 101 S.Ct. 764, 66 L.ed.2d 722 (1981), and no cause to upset their reasoned interpretation of Florida law." (Dissenting Opinion on Bush v. Gore by Associate Justice Ruth Bader Ginsburg, 2000).

All due respect to the late Associate Justice Ruth Bader Ginsburg, but she truly did not comprehend the rules of federalism to raise constitutional questions about whether a sovereign state has violated a constitutional question. The lone dissenter of the Florida Court, Chief Justice Wells, stood with the voting standard principle above the rest. Wells honestly believed that if the nation continued this farce of constitutional crusade for an electoral dispute through the courts, it would bring a constitutional crisis to our republic. The Pennsylvania Supreme Court did their mortal best to discharge their oath more than the Florida court.

At least this court in present times, did nothing to alter or amend a state law passed by the Pennsylvania General Assembly. They respected the voting standards and procedures of the Keystone State assembly's own legislation.

I truly wonder if Justice Ginsburg were alive today, would she have disavowed a state court's decision to re-write a state's electoral code? If Ginsburg sided with one state court to reset the voting standards, why would she not dissent to have another court reset their standards.

"This Court more than occasionally affirms statutory, and even constitutional, interpretations with which it disagrees. For example, when reviewing challenges to administrative agencies' interpretations of laws they implement, we defer to the agencies unless their intent of Congress." *Chevron v. U.S.A., Inc.,* 467 U.S. 837, 843, 104

I truly wonder if Justice Ginsburg were alive today, would she have disavowed a state court's decision to re-write a state's electoral code? If Ginsburg sided with one state court to reset the voting standards, why would she not dissent to have another court reset their standards.

S.Ct.2778, 81 L.Ed.2d 694 (1984). We do so in the face of the declaration in Article I of the United States Constitution that "All legislative powers herein granted shall be vested in a Congress of the United States." Surely the Constitution does not call upon us to pay more respect to a federal administrative agency's construction of *federal law* than to a state high court's interpretation of its own state law. And no uncommonly, we let stand state court interpretations of federal law with which we might disagree. Notably, in the habeas context, the Court adheres to the view that "there is 'no intrinsic reason why the fact that a man is a federal judge **137** should make him more competent, or conscientious, or learned with respect to [federal law] than his neighbor in the state courthouse." (Dissenting Opinion on Bush v. Gore by Associate Justice Ruth Bader Ginsburg, 2000).

The late Justice Ginsburg stated that in her 2000 dissent that our principled document does not call onto them to review a federal administrative agency's own enforcement interpretation or to a state high court's interpretation of its own law. But the Court was asked in this 2000 electoral case to review the unconstitutional, rogue and arrogant Florida high Court's decision to alter Florida's electoral standards and law.

The Court has been established to review whether the federal acting agency or the sovereign state fully interpreted their laws based on the Constitution. We are here to discuss the Florida electoral law standard of voting performed on November 3, 2000.

It is basically not the job of the courts to take up electoral issues, but because it went too far in its constitutional overreach. The Supreme Court had to interject in this debacle. This electoral dispute should have gone to the state legislature. In today's political climate, many Americans are ignorantly unaware, or they do not want to follow proper constitutional parliamentary procedure. I was constitutionally enthusiastic that the Keystone State's high court did not drag the 2020 elections into another 2000.

The Pennsylvania high court in 2020, did not re-write a law, rather it interpreted it as it was written and with accordance to Article II. Therefore, the Court did not take up any suits regarding the election of 2020. They knew that there was no violation of equal protection in the voting booth. And if they had any violations, there needed to be proof. In Florida, the petitioner George W. Bush argued a violation of how they were casting votes that were not being punched through in accordance with Florida electoral law.

Let us bring in Justice Ginsburg's own version of an equal protection violation, to what she believes she saw in the 2000 election.

"I agree with Justice STEVENS that petitioners have not presented a substantial equal protection claim. Ideally, perfection would be the appropriate standard for judging the recount. But we live in an imperfect world, one in which thousands of votes have not been counted. I cannot agree that the recount adopted by the Florida court, flawed as it may be, would yield a result any less fair or precise than the certification that preceded that recount." (Dissenting Opinion on Bush v. Gore by Associate Justice Ruth Bader Ginsburg, 2000).

If Justices Ginsburg and Stevens believed that there was no violation of the equal protection clause in the counting and re-counting of ballots on non-specified standards set by a state court, and not by the state assembly. Our now Republic's interpretative constitutional institution is at a complete loss. The Florida Court was discarding counted ballots and counting uncounted ballots that were not fit to that of Florida's standard of voting.

We do not live in an imperfect world. We do live in a more perfect union with independent sovereign states that make up this American republic. And within these sovereign states lies the principle guiding light that lights up the sky to guide our rules and laws to make this a more perfect union. That guiding light is the American Constitution. The American Constitution sets the rules (of federalism) for the states to enforce them without contradiction, nor intervention from the national government or other states.

"Even if there were an equal protection violation, I would agree with Justice STEVENS, Justice SOUTER, and Justice BREYER that the Court's concern about "the December 12 deadline," *ante*, at 533, is misplaced. Time is short in part because of the Court's entry of a stay on December 9, several hours after an able circuit judge in Leon County had begun to superintend the recount process. More fundamentally, the Court's reluctance to let the recount go forward—despite its suggestion that "[t]he search for intent can be confined by specific rules designed to ensure uniform treatment," ante, at 530—ultimately turns on its own judgment about the practical realities of implementing a recount, not the judgment of those much closer to the process." (Dissenting Opinion on Bush v. Gore by Associate Justice Ruth Bader Ginsburg, 2000).

To burst the imaginary bubble of the late Justice Ginsburg. There was a violation of the equal protection clause. Because the Florida Court declared to set a deadline to count uncounted ballots and establish new precedence, this case did have to reach the high court to be discussed on the value of equal protection.

Justice Ginsburg was more inclined to set a recount with new principles rather than to set a recount based on the current principles set by the appropriate entity, the legislature. "To ensure uniform treatment." What did she mean by that? "To ensure uniform treatment" to the new standards set by the state court or "to ensure uniform treatment" to the standards set by the state legislature, an entity elected by the people. I guess that the late Justice Ginsburg meant to bypass any given law passed by its proper parliamentary procedure and adopt new laws by an improper parliamentary procedure by achieving this unconstitutionality procedure in her desired timeline. Her dissent was indeed a bias vote for Albert C. Gore.

"Equally important, as Justice BREYER explains, *post*, at 556 (dissenting opinion), the December 12 "deadline" for bringing Florida's electoral votes into 3 U.S.C. Section 5's safe harbor lacks the significance the Court assigns it. Were that date pass, Florida would still be entitled to deliver electoral votes Congress *must* count unless both Houses find that the votes "ha[d] not been...regularly given." 3 U.S.C. Section 15. The statute identifies other significant dates. See e.g., Section 7 (specifying *144 December 18 as the date electors "shall meet and give their votes"); Section 12(specifying "the fourth Wednesday in December"—this year, December 27—as the date on which Congress, if it has not received a State's electoral votes, shall request the state secretary of state to send a certified return immediately). But none of these dates has ultimate significance in light of Congress' detailed provisions for determining, on "the sixth day of January," the validity of electoral votes. Section 15." (Dissenting Opinion on Bush v. Gore by Associate Justice Ruth Bader Ginsburg, 2000).

The high court of Florida gave state and local officials a deadline to bring up any kind of votes just six days before Florida's state electors would meet to count their votes. And within that deadline was concocted a revised standard of voting for the state of Florida.

That is one of piece of information, our esteemed Justice Ginsburg left out in her dissent. The electoral deadline for the collection of the state electors were set to count the ballots that were processed within the current legal statute voting standard set by the (Florida) state legislature and not by another governing entity.

In 2020, our esteemed president of the United States wanted to have another governing entity determine the elections. And the popular despot of supporters who once voted for the petitioner George W. Bush and against the Florida high court's decision are now here with the attitude that the Democrats had in 2000. This is truly the evils of a two-party system. It is filled with hypocrisy, lies and deceit. The two-party system has completely disavowed the Founding Fathers' Constitution and replaced it with its own constitution.

"The Court assumes that time will not permit "orderly judicial review of any disputed matters that might arise." *Ante*, at 533. But no one has doubted the good faith and diligence with which Florida election officials, attorneys for all sides of this controversy, and the courts of law have performed their duties. Notably, the Florida Supreme Court has produced two substantial opinions within 29 hours of oral argument. In sum, the Court's conclusion that a constitutionally adequate recount is impractical is a prophecy the Court's own judgment will not allow to be tested. Such an untested prophecy should not decide the Presidency of the United States. I dissent." (Dissenting Opinion on Bush v. Gore by Associate Justice Ruth Bader Ginsburg, 2000).

I have doubted the faith of election officials, attorneys from all sides of this debacle. When individuals and entities ignore the present law and construct their own law to fit to their own narrative to appease the mob is unfaithful and dishonest.

It is quite simple; the state legislature of Florida made the voting standard quite clear. The ballot was supposed to be penetrated and anything but a "dimple" is too be disavowed. The same issue arose in Pennsylvania in 2020, where their state legislature accepted the mail-in ballots as their voting standard procedure. Just because other states do not like it, does not mean they need to meddle. That is the beauty of the rules of federalism and with accordance to the equal protection of the Constitution's Fourteenth Amendment. If any of the proper, legal voting standard ballots are being discarded or not counted, that is a serious constitutional violation. But that is a different topic of discussion that we have not yet witnessed a case, roughly after 1965.

That is where judicial review by the court comes to play. Honestly, you cannot bring judicial review to an issue if the state has not applied it to be an issue.

Since the Florida high court gave the state of Florida a new voting standard procedure, I do attest that the petitioner George W. Bush does have a legal claim. The Court granted for state, county, and local officials to count ballots that were already penetrated but also to count ballots that have been dimpled. Dimpled ballots were not within Florida's procedure. And the manner of counting ballots was to be performed with machine recounts. But the court installed hand recounts, which was not in the current procedure passed by the legislative entity.

The high court of the land never disavowed recounts to be performed. They only disavowed recounts that were not acceptable to the Florida law and with the Article II of the national Constitution. I truly wonder if the 2020 elections were indeed sent to the high court of the land if Justice Ginsburg would still align with partisan politics or contradict her opinion.

This 2000 case should have never seen the light of day in any court's jurisdiction. If Vice President Al Gore was wanting to seek a proper recount procedure and voting standard. Then it would have been constitutionally wise for him to petition the Florida state legislature to make the proper amendments to the current law. The same applies to President Trump. But they sought the easy way out and tried to change the law to satisfy their own selfish egos and against the republic's rules of federalism. I dissent on Justices Stevens' and Ginsburg's dissent because they played partisan politics while not applying the rule of federalism onto the sovereignty of the state of Florida. The high court in 2000 respected the sovereignty of the state, in this case Florida.

I then applaud the Supreme Court for not taking up any case involving the 2020 presidential election. For once, the high court of the land respected the sovereignty of the states —in this case Pennsylvania. Federal government entities must respect the sovereignty of the states, if those entities respect the federalism principle that is the Constitution.

Article II, Section 1, Clause 2 still stands in favoring the republic. The right of the sovereign states to be allowed to pass any law that favors their state. But again, I repeat any action must be in strict accordance with the national Constitution. God save the American republic and the sovereign states that hold it together!

Since 1965, a vote has not been denied. They have been casted. The question here are voters following the procedure and standards set in place? This is what happened in Florida in 2001. The Florida State Legislature set the voting standard and procedure of "punching through the ballot". Voters were given instructions in how to line up their ballot. It is the voter with the common sense that they have, to see their ballot being casted. In Pennsylvania, 2020, they set the standard of ballot boxes in which then-President Trump claimed voter fraud with no evidence. Sovereign states have learned their lesson not to oppress and suppress the vote. But as far as setting counting standards and procedures, it remains in the constitution.

I stand with the sovereign States of our American Republic and still stand with Article II, Section 1, Clause II.

> "As any true American will tell you, it
> is the independence of our sovereign
> States that keeps us free."

It has been twenty-two years since the decision of *Bush v. Gore*. After the Trump v. 2020 mayhem. The so called "We the People" have forgotten the principles of federalism and the power that their sovereign states hold. The power these sovereign entities hold over the national government regarding elections.

This nation was not established and should never set to establish to have a national electoral regulatory standard in any elections. A national electoral standard for all fifty sovereign states is not why and how this republic was formed.

As I do not agree with when the Trump team asked the Supreme Court to step in and decide the 2020 elections to disavow the Pennsylvania, Wisconsin, and Georgia standards. Also, that they asked for those standards to be matched to the standards of Texas. I agree States' standards copying other States' standards, but not by judicial decree. I am so adamantly opposed that the national Congress tried to dictate a national electoral standard for all States. As when they tried to pass the "John Lewis Voting Rights Act".

So, the Trump legal cult team and progressives are using the courts to institute their special interests' ideas onto the Constitution and our republic. We have seen various electoral cases hit the high court's dockets to get the "judicial review" attention it craves. And for these individuals to see if one case hits and ruins our beautiful creation of our American republic of sovereign states.

We have now entered the 2024 elections. Disgraced and now convicted felon former president Donald J. Trump is seeking the Republican party nomination for president. We have seen the former president enter judicial pleas for innocence on various crimes regarding the elections of 2020 and on other individual criminal cases against him. Now various sovereign States are seeking to invoke their sovereign right to Article II, Section I, Clause II against the candidacy of former president Trump. They even sought to pursue to remove Trump with invoking a section of the Fourteenth Amendment. But I knew that was going to be achievable.

To this day and age, we are continuously seeking to answer this question as to what entity should regulate electoral standards. Should the states have this power, or is preempted towards the federal courts, or to the national congress?

Thought this question was answered in 1824, 1876, and 2000, and 2020. In those last four elections that I discussed in this book. We did not have to involve the courts. The national house of representatives got involved correctly and constitutionally. The house of our national congress was not disputing the electoral standards of those three elections. They were disputing and trying to choose a new president because neither candidate obtained a majority of the electoral vote. You heard me, it was the electoral vote, not the popular vote. This country was never founded on democratic electoral values. This nation was founded on republic electoral values.

Then came the election of 2000, George W. Bush v. Albert S. Gore. This election came down to the State of Florida's twenty-five electoral votes. Despite of who was obtaining the majority of the unimportant popular vote, there was a discrepancy towards Florida's state electors. Therefore, neither of the four national candidates obtained the majority of the electoral votes.

Instead of this election going to get resolved by the nation's house of representatives as it is within the constitution. It was being curtailed through the judicial process system of this nation.

Unfortunately, this was the first election in modern-day history in where the popular vote made more standing than the electoral vote. Where the Gore team were advocating "the right of votes to be counted, not the right to vote."

According to the Fourteenth Amendment, all American citizens have this special right to vote, I am not disputing this fact. What the Fourteenth Amendment does not have is the protection of the federal government for electoral counting standards and procedures. That protection is left up to the sovereign States to decide, regulate, and enforce. Whether its set up by the state legislature or the state legislature grants this power to the state courts. It is a power retained by the States.

The high court of this land made the ruling that the Florida standard was retained by the state legislature, and that of the court had no right to alter, change, or amend the current electoral standard. Plus, the high court made it known that this electoral ruling was only going to count once, and no other election would make it to the supreme court dockets.

Trumpism v. Federalism and
the Supreme Court

Article I, Section IV, Clause I

"The Times, Places and Manner of holding Elections for Senators and Representatives, shall be prescribed in each State by the Legislature thereof; but the Congress may at any time by Law make or alter such Regulations, except as to the Places of chusing [sic] Senators.

Article II, Section I, Clause II

"Each State shall appoint, in such Manner as the Legislature thereof may direct, a Number of Electors, equal to the whole Number of Senators and Representatives to which the State may be entitled in the Congress: but no Senator or Representative, or Person holding an Office of Trust or Profit under the United States, shall be appointed an Elector.

The election of 2016, where the New York upset known as Donald J. Trump won that election. He won it, not by the popular vote but by the electoral vote. Trump lost the popular vote to Hillary Clinton. The only people that claim voter fraud at that time were the liberal progressives. I cannot expect any better from the liberal progressive movement in partaking in populist ideals based on an imaginary popular supremacy of law.

I did not even call the 2016 election a fraud because it was correctly decided by the electoral college and with each state electors.

Then came the 2020 elections where the electoral college were going to decide to give Donald Trump another term of office or give it to former Vice-President Joseph Biden.

The electoral college and the popular vote were fully decided to give it to Joe Biden to be the next nation's president. Again, I did not partake to call this election into a fraud or partake to proceed in chanting the famous MAGA line of "Stop the Steal." This time the ones chanting "fraud" were not the liberal progressives, but actual republicans that were denying the Constitution to protect a populist wannabe demagogue.

It was unfortunate that a pandemic of a disease known as COVID-19 made it campaign news for the election of 2020. But it is, what it is, and instead of the federal government regulating electoral standards, President Trump signed an executive order granting the sovereign States the right to initiate legislation in establishing mail-in ballots.

States do not need any permission from the federal government, so what Trump did is not only irrelevant but unconstitutional. But in today's national executive powers, we have treated executive orders as ordinary legislative directives.

As different States enacted different mail-in ballot standards. The results were coming back and unfortunately the electoral and populist votes based on those ballots favored the challenger, Joe Biden.

Of course, to the incumbent in the race was not too partial towards the results. He then decided to challenge the various results in States where the "electoral" votes were granted to Biden.

Henceforth, here we are in this debacle where Donald Trump started useless and incoherent fights with no evidence or facts that his election was ever stolen. He and his MAGA cronies on Capitol Hill and off the Hill began filing lawsuits against several States that gave the win, a small win but nevertheless made Joseph Biden the winner.

The state of Texas and part of their congressional delegation were petitioning the high court to put a stop on the electoral certifications from Wisconsin, Pennsylvania, Michigan, and Georgia.

It is fortunate to have, I believe an unpredictable court nowadays. The high court unanimously decided that the sovereign State of Texas lacked standing to sue the sovereign State of Pennsylvania in how that state conducts their elections, *Texas v. Pennsylvania*, 2020.

Can California sue the state of Idaho for not enforcing federal gun laws? The answer is no just as states cannot sue other states' electoral laws and for them to apply their own laws.

The high courts of Wisconsin and Pennsylvania sought constitutional wisdom to recognize the mail-in ballot law as an appropriate legislation that was approved by their respective state legislature. It was presented by their state legislature because of the Trump executive order.

> "Our consideration is limited to the
> present circumstances, for the problem
> of equal protection in election processes
> generally presents many complexities."
>
> (Per Curiam of Bush v. Gore, 2000).

The Supreme Court did not decide a winner on the 2000 elections and henceforth they did the correct thing and stayed out of the 2020 elections.

But bottom line, the election of 2020 is long and over. Trump lost, Biden won, and the real winner is the electoral college. The electoral college, the last, surviving establishment of pure republic principles chose the winner as they have been doing it for over 200 years. Now we must face a new election.

As we came to the end of 2023 and entered 2024, a new year. This republic enters an extremely critical election season. A test of Federalism versus Trumpism. A test for constitutional values versus greed and corruption under the principles of a madman.

With Trump's wild, illusive, and false statements from 2020 and now entering 2024. I worry for the sanctity and sanity of the American republic. Now do not get me wrong, I also worry with candidates like the incumbent president, and candidates into the ring like Nikki Haley; Chris Christie; Ron DeSantis; and Vivek Ramaswamy. Because sadly, everybody entering the realm of national politics are only thinking in how to expand the general government of the United States.

Also, nowadays, most individuals, male, and female, born from 1965 to 2000, learn about American politics under the curriculum of social studies and not through civics. Therefore, they are not well versed in something called federalism. They have been raised at home and at school that "all" legislative and/or executive directives come from the nation's capital, Washington City.

There are certain directives belonging to the national government. Electoral directives, mainly electoral standards are not enumerated to the federal government, they are enumerated to the States.

Colorado is the first state in 163 years that has removed a candidate from their ballot. There is nothing unconstitutional with this type of ruling or directive. Norma Anderson, former state senator of Colorado, filed a suit to bar Donald J. Trump from the Colorado electoral ballot. As stated in the Colorado electoral code. Norma Anderson, also known to anyone who ever has met her in the halls of the Colorado legislative assembly as "the Dragon Lady." If nothing scared this woman, then Donald Trump should be afraid of this woman.

Ever since the adoption of this second Constitution in 1787, the sanctity of state powers where it pertains to electoral codes and standards has been kept solely to the States and against from being infringed by federal governmental powers.

"But does the U.S. Constitution authorizes states to assess the constitutional qualifications of presidential candidates? We conclude that it does." (Norma Anderson, et. al., v. Jena Griswold, Per Curiam decision on December 19, 2023).

I also conclude that it does as well. The Colorado ruling does make its full argument on the qualifications of a candidate to be removed in the Fourteenth Amendment. That is fine and great, but there is something greater than a Fourteenth Amendment, Section Three challenge to bar Donald J. Trump from a ballot. That greater power of the States enacted in Article II, Section I, Clause II in the federal Constitution.

Back before the establishment of such an amendment known as the Fourteenth, sovereign States had this power and still do, and for Trump and his MAGA cronies to disavow it is wrong. I may not agree what various southern states did in the election of 1860, but I must respect the wish of every sovereign State to do it. Abraham Lincoln, the candidate for president of that election was removed from the ballots in many southern states.

Whether you agreed or disagreed with Lincoln's platforms or Trump (non-existent) platforms. Each state has been granted the power to oversee their elections for their safety and sanity of their citizens as stated in Article II.

"States exercise these powers through "comprehensive and sometimes complex election codes," regulating the registration and qualification of voters, the selection and eligibility of candidates, and the voting process itself. *Andersen v. Celebrezze*, 460

U.S. 780, 788 (1983) (*"Celebrezze"*); see also, e.g., Section 1-4-501(1), C.R.S. (2023) (setting qualifications and well-explored in the U.S. Supreme Court case law." (Norma Anderson, et. al., v. Jena Griswold, Per Curiam decision on December 19, 2023).

A state does not need to explain their electoral codes to any federal government official. If they are not violating that voters' or candidates' civil rights. As far as I know, no state has ever done that or even proved that intent.

The Colorado high court are following their own state electoral code and found reasonable doubt to exclude Donald J. Trump off their ballot. But I will get to display my disappointment in the American people in how they picked their battle to remove Donald J. Trump from the ballot in the Centennial State.

"Under Article II, Section I, (Clause II), each state is authorized to appoint presidential electors "in such Manner as the Legislature thereof may direct." U.S. Const. art. II, sec. I, cl. II. So long as a state's exercise of its appointment power does not run afoul of another constitutional constraint, that power is plenary. *Chiafalo v. Washington*, 140 S. Ct. 2316, 2324 (2020); *McPherson v. Blacker*, 146 U.S. 1, 25 (1892)." (Norma Anderson, et. al., v. Jena Griswold, Per Curiam decision on December 19, 2023).

Supreme Court based their opinions to protect the integrity of the constitution. Sometimes the high court has it right and sometimes they have it wrong. But in the end, we mut abide by their decision to maintain the peace across this union of sovereign States. That peace is to maintain the sanctity of sovereignty for their electoral codes.

In the cases of state's own electoral codes and standards, the high court has sided on the side of federalism and state sovereignty.

Regarding the case of *McPherson v. Blacker*, 1892, they unanimously decided as is. "The Fourteenth Amendment to the U.S. Constitution does not require state legislatures to appoint their electors in the Electoral College on the basis of the popular vote. State legislatures have "plenary" power to allocate their electors however they want."

Popular vote is a vote for the demagogue's ego, who is running for president. If the Framers chose to voice a popular demand, then they would have made this nation into a democracy. But in the end, the popular vote is incoherent and irrelevant in the election of the chief executive for the federal government.

States are not denying their citizens' right to vote. Nowhere in their opinion is the State of Colorado infringing upon that right. The citizens of Colorado will still be allowed to give their vote, and the electors theirs, it's just that their choices have been shrunk to just once less candidate.

"And nothing in the U.S. Constitution expressly precludes states from limiting access to the presidential ballot to such candidates. See *Lindsay v. Bowen*, 750 F. 3d 1061, 1065 (9th Cir. 2014)." (Norma Anderson, et. al., v. Jena Griswold, Per Curiam decision on December 19, 2023).

"Moreover, several courts have expressly upheld states' ability to exclude constitutionally ineligible candidates from their presidential ballots. See id., (upholding California's refusal to place a twenty-seven-year-old candidate on the presidential ballot); *Hassan v. Colorado*, 495 F. App'x 947, 948-49 (10th Cir. 2012) (affirming the Secretary's decision to exclude a naturalization citizen from the presidential ballot); *Socialist Workers Party of Ill., v. Ogilvie*, 357 F. Supp. 109, 113 (N.D. Ill. 1972) (per curiam) (affirming Illinois's exclusion of a thirty-one-year-old candidate from the presidential ballot.) (Norma Anderson, et. al., v. Jena Griswold, Per Curiam decision on December 19, 2023).

There have been multiple cases in local and state courts where Article II stands higher than any candidate. Yet, the high court of the land has refused to take these cases. I believe the nine justices are quite aware that they would be going against the constitution and its Article II.

Alina Habba, spokesperson for the Trump legal team is looking to apply "privilege under law" towards Donald J. Trump.

> "I think it should be a slam dunk in the supreme court. I have faith in them. You know, people like Kavanaugh, who the president went through hell to get into place. He'll step up. Those people will step up, not because they're pro-Trump, because they're pro-

law and pro-fairness." Alina Habba on Fox News Hannity show, January 4, 2024.

What is the constitution got to do with fairness? The constitution is not here to play nice or mean. It plays whatever is dictated within the enclosed document. It is perfectly written that states have this advantage, and the federal high court has no say in the matter.

The Justices of the high court are not here to play favoritism among citizens. Just ask the late Justice Ruth B. Ginsburg. Former President Clinton appointed her to the high court in 1993. A case against the president in 1996 came about and in where President Clinton expected her to vote on his side. What a disappointment was it for him to see her side with the Constitution and not with the president. The Supreme Court must apply the RGB precedent, if the then-the former president can be banned by a sovereign State's ballot.

"As then-Judge Gorsuch recognized in Hassan, it is "a state's legitimate interest in protecting the integrity and practical functioning of the political process" that "permits it to exclude from the ballot candidates who are constitutionally prohibited from assuming office." 495 F. App'x 1t 948." (Norma Anderson, et. al., v. Jena Griswold, Per Curiam decision on December 19, 2023).

Let us all hope that Justice Gorsuch keeps his word to the constitution and not to a president. It is the state's interest under Article II, and not the federal government in this case. It is a state's interest to protect the honesty and ethical process of the sovereign State's electoral standards. According to then-Judge Gorsuch, the constitution does grant the states to remove any person from being added to a ballot. But Justice Gorsuch did not specify how a sovereign State can remove a candidate from their ballot.

"The question then becomes whether Colorado has exercised this power through the Election Code. We conclude that it has." (Norma Anderson, et. al., v. Jena Griswold, Per Curiam decision on December 19, 2023).

We have reached the same conclusion and not quite agreed with this decision.

The answer should all be quite clear for all constitutional Americans out there.

"Section 1-4-1204(4) is Colorado's vehicle for advancing these state interests." (Norma Anderson, et. al., v. Jena Griswold, Per Curiam decision on December 19, 2023).

This electoral law is the vehicle that is driving across the borders of Colorado. The driving force is Article II. I hate to be so redundant, but I need to make it clear to my followers and readers. That nobody, not Trump, or anybody, can interrupt this procedure, and if they do, they are damaging the integrity and sanctity of our constitutional American republic of sovereign States.

The Fourteenth Amendment is just a reason behind the several States filing challenges from

Trump being removed from their ballots. The way Colorado filed, and other states followed suit is not the constitutional way. By using a Fourteenth Amendment challenge, you are encouraging the federal government to encroach on your sovereign State rights and powers.

As Colorado was the first state to bar Trump from the ballot, other states followed suit. Maine under the directive of the Secretary of State Shenna Bellows introduced this proposal to remove Trump from their ballots due to section 3 of the contested amendment.

After both states issued these electoral directives, more states followed their lead.

- Arizona: Trump has faced a challenge in the crucial swing state of Arizona filed by Republican presidential candidate John Castro. But U.S. District Judge Douglas Rayes ruled earlier this month that the challenge has no "standing" because Castro is "not genuinely competing" with Trump for votes in the GOP primary. Castro has filed other legal challenges to Trump's candidacy across the country, but his presidential campaign has not gained traction. "After careful consideration, the Court finds that this case must be dismissed for lack of subject-matter jurisdiction because Castro lacks standing to bring his claim," Rayes ruling reads.

- California: On Wednesday, California Lieutenant Governor Eleni Kounalakis wrote a letter to Secretary of State Shirley Weber urging her to "explore every legal option" to remove Trump from the ballot, citing the Colorado case. "California is obligated to determine if Trump is ineligible for the California ballot for the same reasons described in [Anderson v. Griswold]. The Colorado decision can be the basis for a similar decision here in our state.

- Michigan: Michigan, a battleground state, has also considered a challenge to Trump's candidacy. But the state's Court of Appeals has allowed him to remain on the primary ballot, rejecting challenges to his candidacy.

- Minnesota: Minnesota's Supreme Court similarly ruled that the Republican Party can decide which candidates can appear on the primary ballot. However, the Court also noted that plaintiffs could file a separate challenge after the August 13 primary should Trump win the nomination for the general election.

- Rhode Island: An attempt to remove Trump from the Republican primary ballot failed in Democratic Rhode Island, where U.S. District Court Chief Judge John McConnell, Jr., determined that Castro did not prove he was a "direct and current competitor at the time that he filed his complaint" and could therefore not prove injury.

- Other States where Trump faces ballot challenges. Lawsuits have been filed in several other states: Alaska, Nevada, New Jersey, New Mexico, New York, Oregon, South Carolina,

Texas, West Virginia, Wisconsin, Wyoming, Vermont, and Virginia.

(Full List of States Wanting to Kick Trump off Ballot and Where Cases Stand, Newsweek, Andrew Stanton, weekend staff writer, December 21, 2023).

I am going to digest the individual state's challenges against Trump. I am going to list what is wrong with their challenges and why there is absolutely no mention of Article II, Section I, Clause II. This is the sovereign state's right and privilege to remove candidates from their electoral standards and ballots.

- Arizona: The person who filed the challenge in Arizona did not truly base any legal argument to remove Donald Trump from the ballot. Most of the states were not applying fully the Article II and only applying the argument of a Fourteenth Amendment challenge. If somebody cannot apply this argument and retain the sovereign State's right of this usage, people are less educated than you think. I have no hope for Arizona and the home of the great Senator Barry Goldwater has lost all respect for me.

- California: With California, I have no faith if they are trying to regain their state sovereignty to protect their own electoral code. The government official of that state is trying to investigate and find all legal means to expel Donald Trump off the California ballot. A Fourteenth Amendment, section III challenge is not a suitable fight under Article II's charter. But the charter does not need any excuse, really. This

constitutional article grants any state to regulate and enforce their ballot as they see fit
without any interference from the federal government. This particular "sovereign" state has
never understood the rules of federalism, nor
what it means for a state to retain their sovereignty, away from federal government influence or dependency. (*Gonzales v. Raich*, 2005)

- Michigan: A group filed a challenge to remove
  Donald Trump from their ballot, but a state
  court of appeals denied this challenge and will
  keep Donald Trump on the primary ballot. Even
  though, a primary is orchestrated by the state.
  It is still regulated and enforced by the state.
  Therefore, a state has every right to remove a
  candidate in a primary or general election. The
  challenging group needs to make their case
  strong to stand tall with the charter.

- Minnesota: The high court of this state agreed
  that political party entities can regulate their
  ballots. But they also noted that they can challenge the general election ballot. I quite disagree here because it is the sovereign State that
  regulates ballots, not political parties.

- Rhode Island: The same person that tried to
  remove Trump from the Arizona ballot, is
  doing the same in Rhode Island. This individual is making a mockery of our republic's constitutional electoral standards per states.

This is the very first time in our American republic's history that about 2/3's of all states is trying to

remove a candidate from the presidency. This is no different than in 1860 or in other elections in where states tried to remove a candidate. With just one exception, States are being dependent and using a power belonging to the federal government.

There is nothing strange for a state to do such a thing, as to remove a candidate from their ballot, and quite frankly, it is constitutional. Since the adoption of the constitution in 1787, sovereign States have never lost that right to regulate elections and for people today trying to restrict this right is outright tyrannical.

Followers of Donald Trump tried to seek the national court to intervene on a state-electoral issue. But what can you expect from individuals like Trump? So-called conservative media pundits are putting down the very thought of state sovereignty all the way back to 1860. South Carolina has the right to ban Abraham Lincoln from their ballot, just as Pennsylvania has the same right to have banned John C. Breckenridge from theirs. Colorado still has that right to ban Donald Trump from their ballot, just as Texas has that equal right to ban Joseph Biden from theirs. Lincoln would not have won those South Carolina electoral votes or Breckenridge those Pennsylvania votes, so why would it matter. The same goes for Colorado and Texas.

Are these the same pundits that were once defending the same democrats in protecting their confederate statues? It is called hypocrisy and the pro-Trump movement is just as hypocritical or even worse than a true-Demo-"Dixie"-Crat.

The only time the federal government, the national House of Representatives would get involved in an election is when neither a candidate obtained most of the electoral vote, NOT the popular vote. The national high court need not get involved on state electoral laws. The *Bush v. Gore* debacle should never have reached the high court dockets. It should have reached the national House of Representatives.

I recall the Gore-Lieberman team and the Trump-Pence team in calling the elections, a fraud. The only difference between the two groups is, one wanted to count the votes, while the other wanted to reject the votes.

In an electoral dispute, I rather count the votes than rejecting them. But they need to be counted in accordance with the current electoral state law standard. Yet, the Gore and Trump team wanted to introduce electoral codes from other states to be enforced by the court system and disavow the sovereignty of that affected state. This is not how this republic was established to operate.

Rejecting votes just because a candidate does not like the results is not a good enough reason to overthrow an election, let alone incite an insurrection.

A Candidate who has tried to reject votes has been branded to be intolerable to govern. In other words, a loser. John Adams, one of the framers, lost the election of 1800. He recognized that he, along with Jefferson and Burr did not obtain most of the electoral vote. Therefore, the election went to the U.S. House of Representatives for a vote to decide on a new president. He was a graceful loser of the very first highly contested election in the twentieth century and accepted the results. Unlike before 1824, there were graceful losers, but after 1824, post-Framers world, we have seen arrogant ungrateful losers.

This is the second time that Trumpism has brought the judicial system into a state electoral question. The first time, they were denied and with good standing reason. Now we are here again and because of a little unnerving judicial decree known as "Judicial Review", we are in this debacle. I believe in judicial review where it pertains to items within the federal constitution and its contradictory lawful laws that States provide to the federal government that it brings it to the federal eye.

The respondents of the case, they have their minds are in the right place, but their emotions are in the wrong place. In reading their case, I fully understand that they dislike former President Donald Trump and his style of political positions. But, honestly, they do not need to incite a Fourteenth Amendment challenge against Trump from him to ban him from running for office. They do not have to read so far into the Constitution to ban Trump from an election. I am going to explain their argument and further dive in how they are wrong in using a Fourteenth Amendment challenge. This argument is way better than theirs and it is frankly, not an unknown one, or a secret. It was used in 2000 and made worldwide headlines to implement it.

The petitioners of the case on the other hand contain the same level or more of ignorance as the respondents. The respondents are not denying this challenge. They just focus more on a federal-sponsored article than a state sovereign-sponsored article. While the petitioners quite frankly ignore the main principle and concept of how this republic was formed and needs to be maintained. The petitioners are disavowing the principle of federalism to convey an ego-minded principle of Trumpism. The sovereignty of the States is what keeps our American republic free and independent from the scourge of centralized tyranny. Elections are first on the list to protect the retainment of those state's rights, as well all their people's rights.

I have discussed in detail the very first ungraceful presidential candidate loser that never recognized the winner, in the beginning. Even after the election was constitutionally decided by its proper means. Now we are at again, where the same ungrateful presidential candidate wants to disregard the Constitution made by the States and he wants to install a Constitution to be made by Donald J. Trump.

Let us take the oral arguments first of the petitioners as they spoke first at the Supreme Court.

"A state cannot exclude any candidate for federal office from the ballot on account of Section 3, and any state that does so is violating the holding of Term Limits by altering the Constitution's qualifications for federal office." (Donald J. Trump v. Norma Anderson, 2024, Oral Argument of Jonathan F. Mitchell, Petitioner).

In bringing up the Fourteenth Amendment, Section Three, it is not really a grey area in where a state can ban a candidate from running or holding office. The Fourteenth Amendment is not an amendment for the States. It was made for the protection of the national government and a national protection of citizenry. Where copy is missing from this statement that a true constitutionalist can see, and a true constitutionalist are rare during these fragile republic times. Is that it is Article II, Section I, Clause II gives "a" State, the right to act in such a manner to regulate elections. This is a manner in states regulate their elections, to protect the safety of its citizens.

"A state can exclude any candidate for any office from their ballot on account of Article II, not Section III of the Fourteenth."

A State has more preemptive power in these cases than the national government. Let us never forget that and always remind those with the cult virus known as Trumpism of the constitutional rules of federalism and not the unholy rules of tyranny.

"Griffin was not a precedential Supreme Court decision." (Oral Arguments of Donald J. Trump v. Norma Anderson, 2024, Associate Justice Sonia Sotomayor).

The petitioners are basing their main arguments not on a high court decision but on a lower court decision. A court decision that was never reviewed, heard, or even considered for a supreme court judgment.

The Griffin court case was a case during a time of American history that was darker than the period of Antebellum. This period was known as the

"Black Code era" of the American south. After the Confederate States of America was dissolved, and many southerners did not want to abide to the new Thirteenth Amendment. So, they installed suppressive laws against the newly freed Black American individuals known as "Apprenticeship Laws." A freed black man by the name of Caesar Griffin was convicted of an alleged attempted murder charge in rural Virginia in the late 1860's. The judge, Hugh W. Sheffey, presiding in the case, before he was a judge, was the Speaker to the Virginia General Assembly during the civil war in the Confederate States of America.

The convicted man then sued the judge because his ruling should have been overturned because the judge himself would have been considered an insurrectionist as directed under the Fourteenth Amendment. As the judge was a former confederate official that served in one of the state legislatures of the former Confederate States of America. He would be indeed considered as an insurrectionist but for some reason the Chief Justice of the high court acting as the appellate judge during this trial did not agree with Mr. Caesar Griffin.

Yes, this judge would be considered an insurrectionist given that he disavowed the federal constitution and to boot swore an allegiance to another nation. But as the war ended and States were being re-admitted into the union. Many of these ex-confederates returned to their homes and occupations once again. My question to Mr. Mitchell would be, "Did this individual sign the oath of allegiance to be re-admitted back into the union?"

The answer will be a plain "no." Mr. Sheffey became a judge at the request of the reinstated Virginia General Assembly, just after the Commonwealth was re-admitted into the union. He re-patriated without signing the oath of allegiance. When the southern states were not obeying the new constitutional amendments and creating unconstitutional black code legislations. This case regrettably was a state case and as we know that any challenge made under the Fourteenth Amendment is to be enforced at the federal level, Congress. This lower state argument had no precedent to invoke a Fourteenth Amendment challenge. Congress does, but also regrettably that the membership of fellow congressmen were Republicans that wanted to appease to both the newly freed black men and women but also to the repatriated former confederate rebels coming back into the union. Congress was not going to remove this confederate judge from the bench.

The post-Civil War Courts, or as I like to call it, "The Reconstructive Courts", took it upon themselves to rewrite the Constitution to a newer version of antebellum. Quite frankly, I would never quote anything from the first reconstructive (Chase) court. Maybe, one case, deciding that States have no power to secede, *Texas v. White*, 1869. As my readers and followers know by now is that I am not a secessionist. I do not believe and agree, sovereign States have that power. Once a State enters into this constitutional compact, it is their sovereign duty of that State to find ways to maintain and obey the Constitution, both federal and their State. I am a nullificationist and believe in the power of the State over the central power to be able to maintain that sovereignty and independence.

To hear a lawyer quote and agree with Chief Justice Samuel Chase on a ruling that granted protection to an insurrectionist, especially one that never took the oath of allegiance is very alarming and disheartening. I can see why the high court never heard this case because in the end, it was the right decision. In the end, because if we know how the high court would act, they will act the wrong way and the unconstitutional way.

"So you're relying on a non-precedential case by a justice who later takes back what he said." (Oral Arguments of Donald J. Trump v. Norma Anderson, 2024, Associate Justice Sonia Sotomayor).

"But the key point with Griffin's Case and why it's an important precedent, despite everything Your Honor said, it is not a precedent of the Court, but Griffin's Case provided the backdrop against which Congress legislated the Enforcement Act of 1870 when it first provided an enforcement mechanism for Section 3." (Donald J. Trump v. Norma Anderson, 2024, Oral Argument of Jonathan F. Mitchell, Petitioner).

This case cannot hold any legal water because it is not a supreme precedent. And, furthermore, for the Trump legal time, the petitioners, are spewing nonsense to make themselves look important. Also, for their slick conservative media pundits over at FOX

News, America One, and Tucker Carlson for all to ridicule this lawsuit and spread misinformation.

There is misinformation spread with the statement of Mr. Mitchell. The Griffin case did not spark Congress to initiate legislation that became known as the Enforcement Act of 1870. What sparked Congress after the Griffin Case was to initiate a martial law order in the affected southern states. The Enforcement Act of 1870 was an enforcement law to enforce the Fifteenth Amendment, not the Fourteenth. For the Justices of the high court, not to bring up any corrective statements towards Mr. Mitchell is alarming and disturbing.

If the Trump legal team's main argument is to begin with lies on a lower court ruling that has no supreme court precedent. Also, to spew a false legislative enforcement tale of no legal significance to the Fourteenth.

"...that states had no role in enforcing Section 3 unless Congress was to give them that authority through a statute they passed pursuant to their legislative powers." (Donald J. Trump v. Norma Anderson, 2024, Oral Argument of Jonathan F. Mitchell, Petitioner).

"Well, why would that be an important – why would that be permissible? Because Section 3 refers to the holding of office, not running for office. And so, if a state or Congress were to go further and say that you can't run for office, you can't compete in a primary, wouldn't that be adding an additional qualification for serving for president? You must have been free from this disqualification at an earlier point in time than Section 3 specifies." (Oral Arguments of Donald J. Trump v. Norma Anderson, 2024, Associate Justice Samuel Alito).

After 1865, the meaning of the word, federalism took a new definitive toll and irregularly changed the outcome platform of this republic. I still believe that this Constitution was made by the states to enforce Article II. The newly added amendments is a general government enforcement tool, not a state's enforcement tool. But as I have always stated, just because the civil war was won by the federal government. It does not mean that the very idea of state sovereignty had to be diminished and possible cease to end. If Congress has the authority to ban candidates from holding office under the Fourteenth. Then states have the authority to ban candidates from running for office under Article II.

As Justice Alito points out for the reason of adding qualifications on a state ballot and I say that the ones with authority to add those type of qualifications are the states.

Let us remind our friends on the Trump legal team and the former team of former vice-president Al Gore. The states, themselves have the power to regulate enforce their electoral code, procedures, and standards as they see fit with no regulatory enforcement of the general government.

The petitioners' legal case is not only flimsy but unconstitutional and unprincipled. But I will not side with the respondents' case because it is also unconstitutional and unprincipled to some extent. I still agree with them at least with Article II.

"President Trump's other arguments for reversal ignore the constitutional role of the states in running presidential elections. Under Article II and the Tenth Amendment, states have the power to ensure that their citizens' electoral votes are not wasted on a candidate who is constitutionally barred from holding office." (Donald J. Trump v. Norma Anderson, 2024, Oral Argument of Jason C. Murray, Respondent).

"States are allowed to safeguard their ballots by excluding those who are under age, foreign-born, running for a third presidential term, or, as here, those who have engaged in insurrection against the Constitution, in violation of their oath." (Donald J. Trump v. Norma Anderson, 2024, Oral Argument of Jason C. Murray, Respondent).

"States certainly wouldn't have the authority to remove a sitting federal officer." (Donald J. Trump v. Norma Anderson, 2024, Oral Argument of Jason C. Murray, Respondent).

I could not have said it better myself in describing the state's roles in elections and their standards. This is the first time, somebody in the twenty-first century has stated the Tenth Amendment. The Tenth Amendment is its states' rights doctrine and guidance towards the sovereignty and independence the states strive to perceive away from a tyrannical encroachment of the general government of the United States. In the past, the states had the Articles of Confederation. But that has been long lost and dissolved, and now it is the Tenth.

" – "greater includes the lesser" argument. The – the states have the power, the legislature has the power to choose electors. Granted. But just because there's one authorized means in the Constitution to a particular end does not mean that there's any means to that end. And so I think you're taking the electors argument and bringing it into Section 3, where, as the Chief Justice says, there's just no – and Justice Thomas, there's no historical evidence to support kind of the theory of Section 3, nor the overall – to explain the overall structure of –of the Fourteenth Amendment." (Oral Arguments of Donald J. Trump v. Norma Anderson, 2024, Associate Justice Brett Kavanaugh).

But, unfortunately, the respondents are not using Article II to remove Trump. They are using the Fourteenth Amendment. The people need to stop using this amendment as a constitutional savior. It is not a savior for abortion rights, heterosexual or homo-sexual marriage rights, and now electoral rights to remove candidates.

"And that's all what the Chief Justice Chase focused on a year after the Fourteenth Amendment to say there are difficult questions and you look right at Section 5 of the Fourteenth Amendment, as the Chief Justice said, and that tells you Congress has the primary role here." (Oral Arguments of Donald J. Trump v. Norma Anderson, 2024, Associate Justice Brett Kavanaugh).

I am at least glad that Justice Kavanaugh rec-ognizes the broad power of the federal government under the 14th, not the States. But I see where both the respondents and petitioners have no clue what is entailed in an American civics lesson.

It was established after the bloody conflict of the civil war. When you mix in federal governmental powers and states powers, it creates a bad reaction of plutonium and uranium. Section 5 of the Fourteenth does state that Congress will have the power to enforce the aspect of this amendment. But what Mr. Murray is trying to achieve in his statements is that, even so Congress has this authority to enforce it, states have the authority to enforce any qualifications, and this now includes section 3 of this amendment. WRONG!!

As Congress has the power to define the actions of an individual as labeled in the Fourteenth Amendment. The sovereign States have the power to define the elector qualifications under the broad power of Article II. The respondents are only adding a new qualification, and that is Section 3 of the Fourteenth. The Article II doctrine has broad power as clearly stated by many justices in the past, present and current.

"But maybe put it most boldly, I think that the question that you have to confront is why a single state should decide who gets to be president of the United States. In other words, you know, this question of whether a former president is disqualified for insurrection to be president again is, you know, just say it, it sounds awfully national to me. So whatever means there are to enforce it would suggest that they have to be federal, national means." (Oral Arguments of Donald J. Trump v. Norma Anderson, 2024, Associate Justice Elena Kagan).

"And it's true, I just want to push back a little bit on well, it's a national thing, because this Court will decide it." (Oral Arguments of Donald J. Trump v. Norma Anderson, 2024, Associate Justice Amy Comey Barrett).

This current high court and quite frankly, every single high court decision in our American political history, has sided with the arrogance of the general government of the United States. This court will indeed side with the constitution granting this power to the "arrogant" general government's national Congress and fortunately rightly so.

"Could they do it without Section 3? Could they disqualify somebody for – you know, on whatever basis they wanted outside of the Qualifications Clause? (Oral Arguments of Donald J. Trump v. Norma Anderson, 2024, Associate Justice Neil Gorsuch).

Does a sovereign State have the right to disqualify and set voter standards to protect the integrity of their state and citizens? Within that integrity protection against any dangerous candidate to threaten the well-being and liberty of their residents? The answer to these two questions is a "yes." And third, can a sovereign State do it without the assistance of Section 3? Also, the answer to that question is a definite "yes."

To group these questions together with a more understanding of federalism. Is that the states that make up this union must obey and maintain the guaranteed right in accordance with the federal constitution. That guaranteed right is the blessed Article II that makes this union strong of an indivisible sovereign States.

I know the Trump legal team wants the high court to stand firm on a lower court ruling that makes their case sound legitimate. I would agree with them if this case were a supreme court precedent, but the fact of the matter is that it holds no credibility and must not be applied.

"On – on your point it that it's been dormant for 155 years, I think the other side would say the reason for that Chief Justice Chase's opinion in Griffin's Case to start, which says that Congress has the authority here, not the states." (Oral Arguments of Donald J. Trump v. Norma Anderson, 2024, Associate Justice Brett Kavanaugh).

Quite honestly, States should not invoke anything to do with the Fourteenth Amendment. This tool is not a wise decision to be used by the states. The states have their tool of enforcing from removing candidates from running for office.

If there is anything to do with the Griffin case is that this case is indeed a state issue, not a federal issue. The presiding judge in question was a state official and therefore immune to federal arraignment and prosecution. Hence why, Chief Justice Chase did not proceed anything with this case.

I truly see no similarity to this case and the Trump legal team's attachment to their defense. Yes, the presiding judge was to be classified as an insurrectionist, like Trump. But the judge was a state official, while Trump was a federal official. But the States have a sovereign right, under ethical terms to remove this individual from power. By banning this person (Hugh W. Sheffey) and (Donald J. Trump) from continuing to exercise his right to be seated in elections.

But as I said is that it is alarming that the people of today are not that aware of plain civics lessons and the rules of federalism that plays in our American republic. I despise when jurists pose irrational questions that have no base for logic to our constitutional republic.

"Well, let me ask you a question about whether the power that you've described as plenary really is plenary. Suppose that the outcome of an election for president comes down to the vote of a single state, how the electors of the vote of a single state are going to vote. And suppose that candidate A gets a majority of the votes in that state, but the legislature really doesn't like the candidate A, thinks candidate A is an insurrectionist, so the legislature then passes a law ordering its electors to vote for the other candidate. Do you think the state has that power?" (Oral Arguments of Donald J. Trump v. Norma Anderson, 2024, Associate Justice Samuel Alito).

Even though the states have plenary power as guaranteed under Article II, Section I, Clause II. There is such a thing called common sense to dictate legislative power onto their state. As far as establishing a law to force their electors to vote for a different candidate than candidate A is highly unlikely. Article II does not explicitly state a "spite" clause in the article. What States are lawful to do is set electoral standards to guard off any damaging aspect of their elections towards their citizens. And if they consider Donald J. Trump to be a dangerous aspect of their elections, then so be it. As it was for South Carolina in 1860 against Lincoln, it is for Colorado in 2024 against Trump.

"On what theory? Because Section 3 speaks about disqualification from holding office. You say he is disqualified from holding office from the moment it happens." (Oral Arguments of Donald J. Trump v. Norma Anderson, 2024, Associate Justice Neil Gorsuch).

"Can I just ask you about something Justice Kagan brought up earlier, which is the concern about uniformity and the lack thereof if states are permitted to enforce Section 3 in presidential elections." (Oral Arguments of Donald J. Trump v. Norma Anderson, 2024, Associate Justice Ketanji Jackson).

"I guess my question is why the Framers would have designed a system that would – could result in interim disuniformity in this way where we have elections pending and different states suddenly saying you're eligible, you're not, on the basis of this kind of thing?" (Oral Arguments of Donald J. Trump v. Norma Anderson, 2024, Associate Justice Ketanji Jackson).

To answer Justice Jackson's question along with the hundreds of uneducated Trump supporters…is quite simple to answer. There is no interim or needed disuniformity among our American republic of sovereign States. There is no needed form of judicial review by the federal courts especially where there is no violation within the federal constitution. But when people invoke a federal amendment's challenge, that is where trouble starts. And it will be well-received among the sovereign States.

This is a state (Colorado) issue alone and other states does not need to be dragged into federal courts to deal with a state's own electoral code.

I am not surprised at all with Justice Jackson's question or lack thereof of information among the Constitution and the role the sovereign States play among this union. This problem has become an educational epidemic that we as states have lost control of it. Justice Ketanji Jackson is not to blame here for her blatantly educational ignorance. This is because of the changed programming in our American schools that are now gripped under the claws of an arrogant federal government.

Justice Jackson is from the Generation X of this society. In where this is the first generation of this new educational programming known as "Social Studies" to be our new central government mandated curriculum. While they removed the civics curriculum teaching us the rules of federalism. So, she never undertook the true civics classes of our American republic and instead learned the progressive ideologies of Saul Alinsky, Dr. Benjamin Spock, Margaret Sanger, Rachel Carson, and other progressive ideals that have made dangerous discourse to our educational foundations across America.

The acts of the Courts on electoral issues are in my opinion limited to any present circumstances when it comes to an action against the sovereignty of the state. The act of judicial review on a state's electoral code is a problem that presents a vast of complexities to the rules of federalism. Judicial review should only apply when the government, federal or state, contradicts and violates the constitution against a citizen of that state. The way the court has interpreted this form of judicial activism has been a threat to the constitutional document that lies to protect the integrity and sovereignty of not only the states, but its people.

"Is there a provision for judicial review of secretary of state's action both in Colorado and perhaps what you know about other states?" (Oral Arguments of Donald J. Trump v. Norma Anderson, 2024, Chief Justice John Roberts).

With all due respect to the Chief Justice, but there is no room of provision for judicial review when it comes a state's electoral code. A state is here to protect the electoral integrity of their entity against any one or any group that they deem fit to consider a threat. That integral protection is protected and guaranteed under Article II, and therefore, not subject for court review. But unfortunately, because the State of Colorado used a federal government enforcement amendment, then yes, judicial review is demanded.

To even bring into subject the threat of judicial review to this case is a threat to the federalism liberty across this union of sovereign States.

This case which was brought by the most vile and violent person this nation has ever seen into the high court has opened a Pandora box of dangerous proportions. As the high court did not alter or change Florida's electoral codes in 2000. I pray this court does not alter in any shape or form Colorado's electoral code. If the high court would affirm this case, *United States v. Donald J. Trump*, it is not a win for the Trump legal team. Once again, the ignorance of Trump loses against the Constitution.

To understand this wave of (progressive) populist politics that has plagued our republic. We need to dive into a presidential campaign that in my opinion delved into this unwanted mental syndrome of populism. This presidential election was set in a post-Framers world where new ideas would soon change the founding electoral principles of this, our republic.

The Supreme Court decided to involve themselves in this ruling. This is the first time in American electoral history that the federal court has intervened in a state's election case. I do have to say that I must justify their ruling correctly, not because I am a pro-Trump, but because I am pro-Constitution.

I am a constitutionalist at first, before any political party. At first, I am inclined to state that states do have that right to regulate their ballots under Article II, in by removing a candidate. And they still do but how the respondents prepared their case, made me extremely skeptical and downright upset with them.

I understood what they were trying to use Amendment Fourteenth's Section Three as a qualification for a sovereign State to ban Donald J. Trump from their electoral ballot. But if they would have understood the civil war amendments more clearly, they do not give any powers to the State. These amendments were clearly given power to the national government.

This happens when people are clearly not constitutionally educated. They would simply adapt anything to their case and see if it would stick, and that saddens me.

The respondents as well as every American knows that states have more power than the federal government, if applied correctly. As I will explain how Colorado should have applied their case and to what constitutional article, after I read the ruling on *Trump v. Anderson* and give my analysis and interpretation.

The Fourteenth Amendment, along with the Thirteenth and Fifteenth were amendments added after the bloody civil conflict of the war between the States. You do not have to be an educative wizard, to realize that these articles were crafted and authored with central governance. It was never the intention of these amendment's framers to give one inch of power to the states. The authors knew that the states have their power, and they needed to create a separate power to the national government.

Section 3 of the said amendment states that any one currently holding or about to hold an elected office, and thus having participated in an insurrection are barred from holding that office. To the untrained unconstitutional or ignorant eye, you could make an assumptive case to make a state qualification under this section to remove a candidate by the state legislature. You forgot that the amendment has five sections, and Section Five states that Congress has the authority to regulate this provision, and not the states.

I could give quotes of the amendment's authors in protesting about the urgency to pass this amendment. I am not here to sing praises or quote from former radical republicans. I am here to give you information that states have more power than the general government when it comes to regulating elections. A power that is decreed in the Constitution and cannot be taken away by an act of Congress or federal executive, judicial decree.

"In our federal system, the National Government possesses limited powers; the States and the People retain the remainder." *Bond v. United States*, 572 U.S. 844, 854 (2014). Among those retained powers is the power of a State to "order the processes of its own governance." *Alden v. Maine*, 527 U.S. 706, 752 (1999)." (Per Curiam decision on Trump v. Anderson, 2024).

"In particular, the States enjoy sovereign "power to prescribe the qualifications of their own officers" and "the manner of their election…free from external interference, except so far as plainly provided by the Constitution of the United States, Taylor v. Beckha, 178 U.S. 548, 570-571 (1900)." (Per Curiam decision on Trump v. Anderson, 2024).

Well, I am shocked by this statement made by the high court of its national government. I always expected the arrogance of these bloody (republican) and (democrat) radical jurists to give more power to themselves, and not the States. This goes to the very same statement made by the former senator of South Carolina, in where this Constitution belongs to the States themselves, and a small part belongs to the national government. The small regulatory efforts that belong to the general government of the United States are the three civil war amendments, that includes the Fourteenth.

"Although the Fourteenth Amendment restricts state power, nothing in it plainly withdraws from the States this traditional authority." (Per Curiam decision on Trump v. Anderson, 2024).

The Framers of these amendments knew more about federalism than the legislators and people of today. If they wanted to be arrogant about it, they would have removed Article II, Section I, Clause II and replaced it with a more centrist of regulatory Fourteenth Amendment power. But they did not, they just made those amendments specifically enforced by the national Congress. The guaranteed right of Article II remains, and the states have ample time and liberty to keep enforcing it with the freedom of external interference.

"As an initial matter, not even the respondents contend that the Constitution authorizes States to somehow remove sitting federal officeholders who may be violating Section 3. Such a power would flout the principle that "the Constitution guarantees 'the entire independence of the General Government from any control by the respective States.'" (Per Curiam decision on Trump v. Anderson, 2024).

"The respondents nonetheless maintain that States may enforce Section 3 against *candidates* for federal office. But the text of the Fourteenth Amendment, on it face, does not affirmatively delegate such a power to the States." (Per Curiam decision on Trump v. Anderson, 2024).

"On the other hand, the Fourteenth Amendment grants new power to Congress to enforce the provisions of the Amendment against the States. It would be incongruous to read this Amendment as granting the States the power—silently no less—to disqualify a candidate for federal office." (Per Curiam decision on Trump v. Anderson, 2024).

Even to me, enforcing the Fourteenth Amendment is a guaranteed and stated duty by Congress, not by the individual States. The Framers of these articles never intended to remove any power to the States because that would mean that their home state would lose that same sovereignty as the inflicted southern rebellious states.

As in our federalism republic goes, we cannot give privilege and restrict to another state or take away its state sovereign's rights. Because it will be removed for all.

"The only other plausible constitutional sources of such a delegation are the Elections and Electors Clauses, which authorize States to conduct and regulate congressional and presidential elections, respectively. See Art I, Section IV, cl. I; Art II, Section I, cl. II. But there is little reason to think that these Clauses implicitly authorize the States that authority would invert the Fourteenth Amendment's rebalancing of federal and state power." (Per Curiam decision on Trump v. Anderson, 2024).

"For present purposes, our differences are far less important than our unanimity: All nine justices agree on the outcome of this case. That is the message Americans should take home." (Concurring Opinion on Trump v. Anderson by Associate Justice Amy Comey Barrett, 2024).

It is incredibly happy to see the federal high court give tribute to Article II so that we all can see these powers of the State has not been banished from our American republic of sovereign States.

The high court is right. There is nothing granting each, individual state to use their Article II power to enforce the Fourteenth Amendment's Section 3. To establish a qualifications motive for electoral regulations. Article II is sufficient right enough without the usage of one of the civil war amendments.

I just want to make sure with Justice Barrett's last statement on her concurrence that all nine justices know the true meaning of federalism. The real message we need to broadcast to all Americans is that States are still within their legal and constitutional right to regulate their elections without the infringement from centrist central governance, just as the high court put it.

The concurring opinions of Justices Barrett, Sotomayor, Kagan, and Jackson have the same interpretation. But it appears that Justices Sotomayor, Kagan, and Jackson seem to accept state sovereign rights more than the regular MAGA mob.

"No doubt, States have significant "authority over presidential electors" and, in turn Presidential elections." (Concurring Opinion on Trump v. Anderson by Associate Justices Sonia Sotomayor, Elena Kagan, and Ketanji Jackson, 2024).

From the three most liberal justices of the high court does not seem to deny the guaranteed right of Article II but they also do not deny the federal government right of Section 3 of the Fourteenth Amendment.

"The Reconstruction Amendments "were specifically designed as an expansion of federal power and an intrusion on state sovereignty." (Concurring Opinion on

Trump v. Anderson by Associate Justices Sonia Sotomayor, Elena Kagan, and Ketanji Jackson, 2024).

I like to call them the Civil War Amendments because their main purpose was to establish equality under law for all citizens of this republic of sovereign States. Even though, I would have liked to see the States themselves given this right of citizenry to naturalize and protect their immigration borders and policy. But sadly in 1857, the same high court restricted this right on a racist and unconstitutional ruling. Their statement seems a little bit contradicting because in a previous statement they are not denying the Article II rights of a sovereign State. But here they are introducing federal power preempting state sovereign right.

I must agree with the *Per Curiam* decision as well as the concurring opinions of the three female liberal justices. With Justice Barrett, she just agrees with the decision but does not spell out any state sovereign rights. As the three justices did. It worries me that there are indeed people out there within our republic that want to systematically banish our Constitutional-Given state rights and apply solely federal autocratic power.

As I have always stated before and will continue to keep stating it.

"The might of Article II, Section I,
Clause II is stronger than some MAGA
protesters."

The Constitution is strong and must remain strong to avert tyranny from all political parties, or movements. The Constitution has survived a foreign invasion, a domestic conflict, supremacy inequality, and now an insurrection. It will keep on surviving as long as good citizens respect it, but as well as respect our American union of sovereign States. By respecting the will of that state and respectively the people of that state.

How the General Government Undermines the Electoral Clauses and the Future of Our Republic

Article I, Section IV, Clause I

"The Times, Places and Manner of holding Elections for Senators and Representatives, shall be prescribed in each State by the Legislature thereof; but the Congress may at any time by Law make or alter such Regulations, except as to the Places of chusing [sic] Senators."

Article II, Section I, Clause II

"Each State shall appoint, in such Manner as the Legislature thereof may direct, a Number of Electors, equal to the whole Number of Senators and Representatives to which the State may be entitled in the Congress: but no Senator or Representative, or Person holding an Office of Trust or Profit under the United States, shall be appointed an Elector."

There is a reason why these are independent and sovereign states that make up this union. They are free of intervention and any type of influence from the national government. Within that freedom of national government influence comes the freedom of elections for all those states that have entered this compact. Each state is responsible for their legislative, executive, and judicial actions for their citizens. All state actions must be fair and equal for all regardless of the main qualities their citizens possess.

All citizens have a right to vote as a guaranteed federal government amendment right. There is no disputed claim to that fact. As states are given to protect their citizens the right to vote. The states have also a right to regulate and enforce the counting standards and procedures in their elections.

If there is any violation to their citizens based on any state action, then the action will certainly take place within their state. There is no reason that any state action must be heard at the federal level unless it affects the enumerated powers of the federal government.

There is a thing called judicial review that is the act of reviewing a certain law that may be a probability of a violation. If the courts do find any decisive and legal action under judicial review to challenge the electoral clauses, then they have truly undermined them, but they have dissolved them. Their rightful course of action is to remand these legal cases back to that state legislature for further review it, amend it, or repeal it. I have never heard of judicial "legislative" review, but that is what they are trying to do to our clauses. The courts are not here to act like a self-appointed legislature and re-draft the law to their judicial standards. We will find in this chapter in how the federal government has totally undermined one of the articles that gives the sovereign states the right to be independent from federal or state judicial "legislative" review.

* * *

The right of citizens of the United
States to vote shall not be denied or
abridged by the United States or by any
State on account of race, color, or previous condition of servitude.

"The Voting Rights Act of 1965 is an extraordinary
law." (Dissenting Opinion on Mark Brnovivh, Attorney General of Arizona, Et
Al., Petitioners v. Democratic National Committee, Et Al. by Associate Justice
Elena Kagan, 2021).

It is an extraordinary law. But it shall remain
extraordinary if you do not contradict or circumvent
its purpose to fit your own special interest agenda.
The purpose of the Voting Rights Act of 1965 (VRA)
is to reaffirm the federal government's position on
its newly acquired power of equality voting rights as
guaranteed by the Fifteenth Amendment.

The Amendment is quite clear as how it was written on 1868. It was designed to guarantee the right to
vote for all citizens regardless of race, sex, or class of
servitude. But this act cannot restrict the state's power
to regulate and enforce their elections.

"Never has a statute done more to advance the
Nation's highest ideals. And few laws are more vital
in the current moment. Yet in the last decade, this
Court has treated no statute worse. To take the measure of today's harm, a look to the Act's past must
come first. The idea is not to recount, as the majority
hurriedly does, some bygone era of voting discrimination. See ante, at 2-3. It is instead to describe the
electoral practices that the Act targets—and to show

the high stakes of the present controversy." (Dissenting Opinion on Mark Brnovivh, Attorney General of Arizona, Et Al., Petitioners v. Democratic National Committee, Et Al. by Associate Justice Elena Kagan, 2021).

"In these cases, we are called upon for the first time to apply Section 2 of the Voting Rights Act of 1965 to regulations that govern how ballots are collected and counted. Arizona law generally makes it very easy to vote. All voters may vote by mail or in person for nearly a month before election day, but Arizona imposes two restrictions that are claimed to be unlawful. First, in some counties, voters who choose to cast a ballot in person on election day must vote in their own precincts or else their ballots will not be counted. Second, main-in ballots cannot be collected by anyone other than an election official, a mail carrier, or a voter's family member, household member, or caregiver. (Opinion Brief on Mark Brnovivh, Attorney General of Arizona, Et Al., Petitioners v. Democratic National Committee, Et Al. by Associate Justice Samuel Alito, 2021).

Per the beginning opinion of Justice Alito, the law of the sovereign state of Arizona is quite clear and there is no ambiguity for a show of discriminatory intent.

The question before me is to confirm if this state electoral law contradicts or circumvents the Fifteenth Amendment. Or its affirmed law known as the Voting Act of 1965. The question that I am not seeking is a recount of votes as we saw in the 2000 decision of *Bush v. Gore*. The question that I am seeking is if this law is disavowing votes in this current Arizona's electoral standard. If it is also not violating the federal constitution.

"Despite the ratification of the Fifteenth Amendment, the right of African-Americans to vote was heavily suppressed for nearly a century. States employed a variety of notorious methods, including poll taxes, literacy tests, property qualifications; 'white primar[ies]', and grandfather clause[s].'" Challenges to some blatant efforts reached this Court and were held to violate the Fifteenth Amendment. But as late as the mid-1960s, black registration and voting rates in some States were appallingly low. See South Carolina v. Katzenbach, 383 U.S. 301, 313 (1966)." (Opinion Brief on Mark Brnovivh, Attorney General of Arizona, Et Al., Petitioners v. Democratic National Committee, Et Al. by Associate Justice Samuel Alito, 2021).

"Invoking the power conferred by Section 2 of the Fifteenth Amendment, see 383; City of Rome v. United States, 446 U.S. 156, 173 (1980), Congress enacted the Voting Rights Act (VRA) to address this entrenched problem. The Act and its amendments in the 1970s specifically forbade some of the practices that had been used to suppress black voting." (Opinion Brief on Mark Brnovivh, Attorney General of Arizona, Et Al., Petitioners v. Democratic National Committee, Et Al. by Associate Justice Samuel Alito, 2021).

Most voting suppressions were being unconstitutionally performed in various southern states. But there were also cases of voting suppressions done in various Rocky Mountain states and Southwestern states against the Hispanic and Native American members of our society. But as Justice Alito has detailed the horrible practices that many members of our minority community have endured, I truly do not see any damage here presented against the sovereign state of Arizona.

"Today, the Court undermines Section 2 and the right it provides. The majority fears that the statute Congress is too "radical"—that it will invalidate too many state voting laws. See *ante*, at 21, 25. So the majority write its own set of rules, limiting Section 2 from multiple directions." (Dissenting Opinion on Mark Brnovivh, Attorney General of Arizona, Et Al., Petitioners v. Democratic National Committee, Et Al. by Associate Justice Elena Kagan, 2021).

> Applying emotionality rather than applying the rules of federalism on electoral laws will not get you my sympathy.

"The Voting Rights Act is ambitious, in both goal and scope. When President Lyndon Johnson sent the bill to Congress, ten days after John Lewis led marchers across the Edmund Pettus Bridge, he explained that it was "carefully drafted to meet its objective— the end of discrimination in voting in America." H.R. Doc. No. 120, 89th Cong., 1st Sess., 1-2 (1965). He was right about how the Act's drafting reflected its aim. "The end of discrimination in voting" is a far-reaching goal. And the Voting Rights Act's text is just as far-reaching... But Section 2 of the Act remains, as written, as expansive as ever—demanding that every citizen of this country possess a right at once grand and obvious: the right to an equal opportunity to vote." (Dissenting Opinion on Mark Brnovivh, Attorney General of Arizona, Et Al., Petitioners v. Democratic National Committee, Et Al. by Associate Justice Elena Kagan, 2021).

Applying emotionality rather than applying the rules of federalism on electoral laws will not get you my sympathy.

"As originally enacted, Section 2 closely tracked the language of the Amendment it was adopted to enforce. Section 2 stated simply that "[n]o voting qualification or prerequisite to voting, or standard, practice, or procedure shall be imposed or applied by any State or political subdivision to deny or abridge the right of any citizen of the United States to vote on account of race or color." 79 State. 437." (Opinion Brief on Mark Brnovivh, Attorney General of Arizona, Et Al., Petitioners v. Democratic National Committee, Et Al. by Associate Justice Samuel Alito, 2021).

It took this republic, roughly about one-hundred years to let all citizens enter the voting booth. After 1965, the federal government affirmed its power to bring protection to each and all citizens to vote. Therefore, the sovereign states cannot find way to discriminate the voter because of the color of his or her skin as they enter the voting booth.

What I am trying to find out the question to this issue is if the sovereign state of Arizona found any way to discriminate their fellow citizens and discarded their ballots. Let us remember Article II, Section I, Clause II, that also affirms the sovereign state to appoint their own electors. As they appoint their electors, the State gets to legislate and enforce a voting standard for electoral purposes. And that voting standard must not find its way to discriminate the ballot of the voter.

"The present dispute concerns two features of Arizona voting law, which generally makes it quite easy for residents to vote. All Arizonans may vote by mail for 27 days before an election using an "early ballot." Ariz. Rev. Stat. Ann. Sub-Section 16-541 (2015), 16-542(C) (Cumm. Supp. 2020). No special excuse is needed, Sub-Section 16-541(A), 16-542(A), and any voter may ask to be sent an early ballot automatically in future elections, Section 16-544(A) (2015). In addition, during the 27 days before an election, Arizonans may vote in person at an early voting location in each county. See Sub-Section 16-542(A), (E). And they may also vote in person on election day." (Opinion Brief on Mark Brnovivh, Attorney General of Arizona, Et Al., Petitioners v. Democratic National Committee, Et Al. by Associate Justice Samuel Alito, 2021).

We have now established the current voting standard of Arizona. I see no sign of discrimination towards the voter, do you? The standard is quite clear. The voter can either choose to vote by mail and given 27 days before election day or present himself or herself to the polling place to vote.

"The regulations at issue in this suit govern precinct-based election-day voting and early mail-in voting. Voters who choose to vote in person on election day in a county that uses the precinct system must vote in their assigned precincts. See Section 16-122 (2015); see also Section 16-135. If a voter goes to the wrong to the wrong polling place, poll workers are trained to direct the voter to the right direction. Democratic Nat. Comm. V. Reagan, 329 F. Supp. 3d 824, 859 (Ariz. 2018); see Tr. 1559, 1586 (Oct. 12, 2017); Tr. Exh. 370

(Pima County Elections Inspectors Handbook). If a voter finds that his or her name does not appear on the register at what the voter believes is the right precinct, the voter ordinarily may cast a provisional ballot. Ariz. Rev. Stat. Ann. Section 16-584 (Cum. Supp. 2020). That ballot is later counted if the voter's address is determined to be within the precinct. See *ibid*. But if it turns out that the voter cast a ballot at the wrong precinct, that vote is not counted. See Section 16-584(E); App. 37-41 (election procedures manual); Ariz. Rev. Stat. Ann. Section 16-452(C) (misdemeanor to violate rules in election procedures manual)." (Opinion Brief on Mark Brnovivh, Attorney General of Arizona, Et Al., Petitioners v. Democratic National Committee, Et Al. by Associate Justice Samuel Alito, 2021).

"For those who choose to vote early by mail, Arizona has long required that "[o]nly the elector may be in possession of that elector's unvoted early ballot." Section 16-542(D). In 2016, the state legislature enacted House Bill 2023 (HB 2023), which makes it a crime for any person other than a postal worker, an elections official, or a voter's caregiver, family member, or household member to knowingly collect an early ballot—either before or after it has been completed. Sub-Section 16-1005(H)-(I)." (Opinion Brief on Mark Brnovivh, Attorney General of Arizona, Et Al., Petitioners v. Democratic National Committee, Et Al. by Associate Justice Samuel Alito, 2021).

We have now established the enforcement of the current voting standard of the sovereign state of Arizona. In reading the enforcement statutes for

Trying to prove discriminatory intent in this Arizona case is like Donald J. Trump trying to prove electoral theft intent in the 2020 elections.

these voting standards, I truly do not see any discriminatory intent proposed by the plaintiffs. The voting law standard is quite clear to follow. The voter is giving guidelines to follow to vote, which they must follow accordingly.

"In 2016, the Democratic National Committee and certain affiliates brought this suit and named as defendants (among others) the Arizona attorney general and secretary of state in their official capacities. Among other things, the plaintiffs claimed that both the State's refusal to count ballots cast in the wrong precinct and its ballot-collection restriction "adversely and disparately affect Arizona's American Indian, Hispanic, and African American citizens," in violation of Section 2 of the VRA. *Democratic Nat. Comm. v. Hobbs*, 948 F. 3d 989, 998 (CA9 2020) (en banc). In addition, they alleged that the ballot-collection restriction was "enacted with discriminatory intent" and thus violated both Section 2of the VRA and the Fifteenth Amendment. *Ibid.*" (Opinion Brief on Mark Brnovivh, Attorney General of Arizona, Et Al., Petitioners v. Democratic National Committee, Et Al. by Associate Justice Samuel Alito, 2021).

Arizona's current standard of voting has not shown to me any sign of discriminatory intent. Trying to prove discriminatory intent in this Arizona case is like Donald J. Trump trying to prove electoral theft intent in the 2020 elections. When submitting an intent of voter fraud, the individual truly needs to have concrete and definite evidence to build a case. Emotional support is not enough to bring a suit to the highest court of the land.

"Yet efforts to suppress the minority vote continue. No one would know this from reading the majority opinion. It hails the "good news" that legislative efforts had mostly shifted by the 1980s from vote denial to vote dilution. *Ante*, at 7. And then it moves on to longer has a problem to address—as though once literacy tests and poll taxes disappeared, so too did efforts to curb minority voting. But as this Court recognized about a decade ago, "racial discrimination and racially polarized voting are not ancient history." *Bartlett v. Strickland*, 556 U.S. 1, 25 (2009). Indeed, the problem of voting discrimination has become worse since that time—in part because of what this Court did in *Shelby County*. Weaken the Voting Rights Act, and predictable consequences follow: yet a further generation of voter suppression laws." (Dissenting Opinion on Mark Brnovivh, Attorney General of Arizona, Et Al., Petitioners v. Democratic National Committee, Et Al. by Associate Justice Elena Kagan, 2021).

I am first to recognize that many southern state legislatures were being contradictory and circumventing the federal constitution's Fifteenth Amendment in the late nineteenth and most of the twentieth centuries. They were indeed suppressing various minority voters across the board with excuses like excessive poll taxes; literacy tests; and other unconstitutional regulatory laws.

With the passage of the VRA of 1965, we finally saw that cloud of contradictory laws go away and all citizens regardless of race began to exercise their right to vote with no sense of threat or coercion.

Many veterans of the Civil Rights movement that witnessed violence against black citizens to obtain the right to vote, have remained skeptical of new state electoral laws taking effect. It is quite understandable, but anxiety does not help the cause of equality. They cannot attack every single sovereign state electoral law, just because they assume it is a strict voter suppression law of the segregation days.

If an electoral law that goes into effect, shows no evidence of voter suppression as we saw in the 1950s and 1960s, then that means that all citizens of all walks of American life have exercised their right to vote.

Citizens today has not lost their right to vote. It is quite different when a state determines if that vote should be counted per their standards. A vote is casted but if that vote does not meet the standards of a state electoral code, should it be casted or counted?

"The interpretation set above follows directly from what Section 2 commands: consideration of "totality of circumstances" that have bearing on whether a State makes voting "equally open" to all and gives everyone an equal "opportunity" to vote. The dissent, by contrast, would rewrite the text of Section 2 and make it turn almost entirely on just one circumstance—disparate impact." (Opinion Brief on Mark Brnovivh, Attorney General of Arizona, Et Al., Petitioners v. Democratic National Committee, Et Al. by Associate Justice Samuel Alito, 2021).

"That is a radical project, and the dissent strains mightily to obscure its objective. To that end, it spends 20 pages discussing matters that have little bearing on the questions before us. The dissent provides historical background that all Americans should remember, see *post*, at 3-7 (opinion of Kagan, J.), but that background does not tell us how to decide these cases. The dissent quarrels with the decision in *Shelby County v. Holder*, 570 U.S. 529 (2013), see *post*, at 7-9, which concerned Sub-Sections 4 and 5 of the VRA, not Section 2. It discusses all sorts of voting rules that are not at issue here. See post, at 9-12. And it dwells on points of law that nobody disputes: that Section 2 applies to a broad range of voting rules, practices, and procedures, that an "abridgement" of the right to vote under Section 2 does not require outright denial of the right; that Section 2 does not demand proof of discriminatory purpose; and that a "facially neutral law or practice may violate that provision. See *post*, at 12-20." (Opinion Brief on Mark Brnovivh, Attorney General of Arizona, Et Al., Petitioners v. Democratic National Committee, Et Al. by Associate Justice Samuel Alito, 2021).

Has this Republic truly learned from its past mistakes? Are we now entering a new era of federalism in where all citizens are equal under law?

The wound is still open, but we are trying to heal for the sovereign states to return to their sovereignty with the new norm that is equality. We cannot have drastic measures of sovereign states contradicting and circumventing the federal constitution. And we cannot have an intrusive federal autocracy dictating policy onto the states. We must come to terms that "We are all citizens of this American Republic of sovereign States" and that we must all respect each other.

The creation is quite simple to comprehend. This nation was established a lawful and constitutional nation of sovereign states guided under the principled document known as the constitution. The national Congress can add new amendments that became laws to this document. States must find it in their just and legal minds to follow these new amendments as part of their constitutional compact.

Newly made duties to the national government were the protection and abolition of slavery; equality of all citizens; the right to vote for all citizens. Re-admitted sovereign states after the bloody civil war, had to abide to these newly made duties. But sadly, many states still rebelled, circumvented, and contradicted the federal constitution. Hence, the establishment of the Voting Rights Act of 1965.

The VRA was to bring an end to this rebellion, circumvention, and contradiction of these segregated laws. And it did find a way to end them. Nowhere did you ever see the constant discrimination towards the voters of all sovereign states. But the sovereign and independent states must tread carefully that they do not overstep their bounds.

In 2013, The high Court saw fit to strike a provision of this Act and regain some sovereignty but with the essence of equality which I honestly believe that is what the majority achieved with the decision of *Shelby County v. Holder*, 2013.

"Section 2 of the Voting Rights Act provides vital protection against discriminatory voting rules, and no one suggests that the threat has been eliminated. But Section 2 does not deprive the States of their authority to establish non-discriminatory voting rules, and that is precisely what the dissent's radical interpretation would mean in practice. The dissent is correct that the Voting Rights Act exemplifies our country's commitment to democracy, but there is nothing democratic about the dissent's attempt to bring about a whole-sale of transfer of the authority to set voting rules from the States to federal courts." (Opinion Brief on Mark Brnovivh, Attorney General of Arizona, Et Al., Petitioners v. Democratic National Committee, Et Al. by Associate Justice Samuel Alito, 2021).

The Voting Rights Act does exemplify a commitment not to democracy but to equality among our fellow citizenry. Even to this day, our fellow members of the Court fail to grasp the unity of rules that binds our Republic together. The constitution is our document that holds this nation together in unity while maintaining the sense of independence and sovereignty.

The Fifteenth Amendment states that no violation of discrimination shall exist among our citizens. The Voting Rights Act affirms that promise. Ever since passage of this Act, the violations of discrimination have diminished but the scare tactics have increased and that neither shall take place. I would support a federal government intervention in setting up new voting rules. If those rules in question are a threat to the equality of the voter in the intent of discrimination. But would support it through the proper channels of government, which is the legislature, and not via the courts.

For the dissenting majority to initiate a claim of discriminatory intent is crying wolf without presenting the evidence. America has had a dark past of voter discrimination based on race, but I believe we have moved forward and let our sovereign states regain their sovereignty once again with the new set of rules in place. In not to return to that dark place in time of American history.

"But this Court took a different view. Finding that "[o]ur country has changed," the Court saw only limited instances of voting discrimination—and so no further need for preclearance. Shelby County, 570 U.S., at 547-549, 557. Displacing Congress's contrary judgment, the Court struck down the coverage formula essential to the statute's operation. The legal analysis offered was perplexing: The Court based its decision on a "principle of equal [state] sovereignty" that a prior decision of ours had rejected—and that has not made an appearance since. Id., at 544 (majority opinion); see id., at 587-588 (Ginsburg, J., dissenting). (Dissenting Opinion on Mark Brnovivh, Attorney General of Arizona, Et Al., Petitioners v. Democratic National Committee, Et Al. by Associate Justice Elena Kagan, 2021).

"like throwing away your umbrella in a rainstorm because you are not getting wet." (Dissenting Opinion on Shelby County v. Holder by Associate Justice Ruth Bader Ginsburg, 2013).

The constitution, post 1865 gave a new meaning for state sovereignty. But the idea of federalism remained the same. From 1868 to the year that the Voting Rights Act became law, yes, there was misinterpretation of this new meaning. I understand the animosity towards the new present laws being presented in several sovereign state legislatures.

"States and localities put in place new restrictive voting laws, with foreseeably adverse effects on minority voters. On the very day *Shelby County* issues, Texas announced that it would implement a strict voter identification requirement that had failed to clear Section 5. See Elmendorf & Spencer, Administering Section 2 of the Voting Rights Act After Shelby County, 115 Colum. L. Rev. 2143, 2145-2146 (2015). Other states—Alabama, Virginia, Mississippi—fell like dominoes, adopting measures similarly vulnerable to preclearance review. See *Ibid.* The North Carolina Legislature, starting work the day after Shelby County, enacted a sweeping election bill eliminating same-day registration; forbidding out-of-precinct voting; and reducing early voting, including souls-to-the-polls Sundays. (That law went too far even without Section 5: A court struck it down because the State legislators had a racially discriminatory purpose. *North Carolina State Conference of NAACP v. McCrory*, 831 F. 3d 204 (CA4 2016). States and localities redistricted—drawing based seats with at-large seats—in ways guaranteed to reduce minority representation. See Elmerdorf, 115 colum. L. Rev., at 2146. And jurisdictions closed polling places in mostly minority areas, enhancing an already pronounced problem. See Brief for Leadership Conference on Civil and Human Rights et al. as Amici Curiae 14-15 (listing closure schemes); Pettigrew, The Racial Gap in Wait Times, 132 Pol. Sci. Q. 527, 527 (2017) (finding that lines in minority precincts are twice as long as in white ones, and that a minority voter is six times more likely to wait more than an hour)." (Dissenting Opinion on Mark Brnovivh, Attorney General of Arizona, Et Al., Petitioners v. Democratic National Committee, Et Al. by Associate Justice Elena Kagan, 2021).

And yes, several of these new laws where people felt threatened that lost their rights. Just because the Civil War was achieved in a federal government victory, the very thought of the principle for state sovereignty did not have to ceased to exist. New rules of federalism were established for this union of sovereign states to comply. But sadly, people still filled with rage decided not to comply and began to contradict the principled manifest, the Constitution.

Because the ignorance of a few, many others had to suffer the arrogant presence of a meddling federal autocracy. That ended in 1965, sealed the fate of those voter suppression laws and finally set a new era of state sovereignty that opened for this American Republic. The Voting Rights Act of 1965, Section 2 ended the racial and discriminatory intent towards the electorate of the minority community, but it did not end the very idea of state sovereignty.

> "No voting qualification or prerequisite to voting or standard, practice, or procedure shall be imposed or applied by any State or political subdivision in a manner which results in a denial or abridgement of the right of any citizen of the United States to vote on account of race or color." 52 U.S.C. Section 10301(a)."

In reading *Shelby County v. Holder*, I show no discriminatory intent of voting towards the residents of the sovereign state of North Carolina. The State Legislature as guaranteed in Article II, Section, I, Clause II, were setting their rules and standards and applying both the Voting Rights Act and federalism. As we will see in the sovereign State of Arizona, they also were not applying any discriminatory intent. What the Shelby decision did was to strike down a federal overseeing authority pre-clearance (Section 4b) of when a law is passed by a state legislature that does not violate the Act or the Amendment.

I understand the frustration of people that may be inclined to believe of voter suppression and voter discrimination while at the polling place. But way since after 1965, the very idea of that suppression has changed. I genuinely believe that the American Republic is seeing a clear view to move out of that stint of segregation and discrimination. But the sovereign States cannot be inclined to halt to dictate their own sovereign policy by waiting for a response from a centralized autocracy. The Voting Rights Act has good intentions, but we cannot deny the legislative intentions of a sovereign State as stated in Article II to pursue their own laws in accordance with Article II. The playing field (Fifteenth Amendment) is set along with Article II and we, as a Republic of sovereign States need to learn the rules of federalism to be able to play, fairly and equally.

"In light of the principles set out above, neither Arizona's out-of-precinct rule nor its ballot-collection law violates Section 2 of the VRA. Arizona's out-of-precinct rule enforces the requirement that voters who choose to vote in person on election day must do so in their assigned precincts. Having to identify one's own polling place and then travel there to vote does not exceed the "usual burdens of voting." Crawford, 553 U.S., at 198 (opinion of Stevens, J.) (noting the same about making a trip to the department of motor vehicles). On the contrary, these tasks are quintessential examples of the usual burdens of voting." (Opinion Brief on Mark Brnovivh, Attorney General of Arizona, Et Al., Petitioners v. Democratic National Committee, Et Al. by Associate Justice Samuel Alito, 2021).

"Arizona law also mandates that election officials send a sample ballot to each household that includes a registered voter who has not opted to be placed on the permanent early voter list, Ariz. Rev. State. Ann. Section 16-510(C) (2015), and this mailing also identifies the voter's proper polling location, 329 F. Supp. 3d, at 859. In addition, the Arizona secretary of state's office sends voters pamphlets that include information (in both English and Spanish) about how to identify their assigned precinct. *Ibid.*" (Opinion Brief on Mark Brnovivh, Attorney General of Arizona, Et Al., Petitioners v. Democratic National Committee, Et Al. by Associate Justice Samuel Alito, 2021).

The secretary of state's office in Arizona is offering easier access and available information to all voters. To even voters, that English is not their primary language but are citizens and residents of that sovereign state in this republic.

As Section 2 of the VRA currently stands, there should be no discriminatory intent in the sovereign state's electoral law to deny the vote to a citizen of these sovereign states of this Republic on account of race or color or even a language difference.

The dissent was written to try to prove a discriminatory intent, but I would say that the dissent would be in the sense of a contradiction against the rules of federalism.

I see no discriminatory intent in this Arizona electoral law. I see idiocy, ignorance, and lunacy in how the legislators of that sovereign state created this law. I see now why the minority opinion of this court dissented, but they dissented for the wrong reasons. The dissent was written to try to prove a discriminatory intent, but I would say that the dissent would be in the sense of a contradiction against the rules of federalism.

"HB 2023 likewise passes muster under the results test of Section 2. Arizonans who receive early ballots can submit them by going to a mailbox, a post office, an early ballot drop box, or an authorized election official's office within 27-day early voting period." (Opinion Brief on Mark Brnovivh, Attorney General of Arizona, Et Al., Petitioners v. Democratic National Committee, Et Al. by Associate Justice Samuel Alito, 2021).

"Voters may drop off their early ballots at any polling place, even one to which they are not assigned." (Opinion Brief on Mark Brnovivh, Attorney General of Arizona, Et Al., Petitioners v. Democratic National Committee, Et Al. by Associate Justice Samuel Alito, 2021).

"They can also drop off their ballots at any polling place or voting center on election day, and in order to do so, they can skip the line of voters waiting to vote in person. 329 F. Supp. 3d, at 839 (citing ECF Doc. 361, Paragraph 57). Making any of these trips—much like traveling to an assigned polling place—falls squarely within the heartland of "unusual burdens of voting." Crawford, 553 U.S., at 198 (opinion of Stevens, J.). And voters can also ask a statutorily authorized proxy—a family member, a household member, or a caregiver—to mail a ballot or drop it off at any time within 27 days of an election." (Opinion Brief on Mark Brnovivh, Attorney General of Arizona, Et Al., Petitioners v. Democratic National Committee, Et Al. by Associate Justice Samuel Alito, 2021).

This case is not a case of discriminatory intent. This is a case of electoral contradiction of its own laws and standards in Arizona.

I can see where the dissenting minority may get that impression of discriminatory intent towards the voter but that is not further from the truth. It is a clear case of political legislatorial lack of organization. A sheer lack of interest in providing a view of equality voting access to one set of standard but not to the other. The law cannot be unequal in its aspect to show that the said voter can drop the assigned ballot to more than one ballot box location but voting in person must be in the assigned precinct. The legislator or legislators in question that sponsored the legislation should have been called to answer their broad view of law they have written. The law in question, should have ordered to be reviewed by the Arizona legislature, and not decided by judicial review by the high court.

What the dissenting opinion are trying to prove is that because the voter being dismissed from a polling place that is not theirs, especially if that voter is of a minority race or color. The voter in no such way is being denied their right to vote. The law is quite clear that if the voter, regardless of their race or color arrive to a polling place that is not registered to them. They will not be allowed to vote in that place of polling. But the election officials have been instructed to advise them of their correct place as established in their sovereign law. I have not seen that an election official of this state or other states that have denied the voter any information. Any voting information that pertains to their ballot casting information. The voter has not been denied a mail-in-ballot drop-off location. As they can go to any location.

> "No voting qualification or prerequisite to voting or standard, practice, or procedure shall be imposed or applied by any State or political subdivision in a manner which results in a denial or abridgement of the right of any citizen of the United States to vote on account of race or color." 52 U.S.C. Section 10301(a)."

"Those provisions have a great many words, and I address them further below. But their essential import is plain: Courts are to strike down voting rules that contribute to a racial disparity in the opportunity to vote, taking all the relevant circumstances into account." (Dissenting Opinion on Mark Brnovivh, Attorney General of Arizona, Et Al., Petitioners v. Democratic National Committee, Et Al. by Associate Justice Elena Kagan, 2021).

Justice Kagan in her dissent lists the manner of violations that a sovereign State cannot do to deny a ballot to the voter. The esteemed Justice has to comprehend that the law was written at a time in where voter discrimination was at all time high and contradiction. But now, she and the rest of the American Republic must finally come to terms that times are changing and we are trying very hard to move away from that dark cloud of racism and segregation. Yes, there are individuals that have entered the political world filled with a racist cultist mindset trying to undermine, contradict and discriminate the voters of this land. The constitution is stronger than some insurgency.

In detailing Section 2 of the VRA, let us see if Justice Kagan can identify a possible voter discrimination intent in this Arizona's law and case. Let us take the "locations of polling places" within Section 2 and the law in question.

"So, for example, the provision "covers all manner of registration requirements, the practices surrounding registration," the "location of polling places", the times polls are open, the use of paper ballots as opposed to voting machines, and other similar aspects of the voting process that might be manipulated to deny any citizen the right to cast a ballot and have it properly counted." *Ibid.* All those rules and more come within the statute—so long

To this day, the Court has not denied a sovereign State legislature their Article II power and I hope that day never comes into existence.

as they result in a race-based "denial or abridgement" of the voting right." (Dissenting Opinion on Mark Brnovivh, Attorney General of Arizona, Et Al., Petitioners v. Democratic National Committee, Et Al. by Associate Justice Elena Kagan, 2021).

As I have read the Arizona law in question, there is no doubt in my mind that it is not showing any discriminatory of intent towards a denial of polling place access or ballot access. Each voter lives in a designated area of their sovereign State and within that area a precinct.

"And the "denial" or "abridgement" phrase speaks broadly too. "[A]bridgement necessarily means something more subtle or less drastic than the complete denial of the right to cast a ballot, denial being separately forbidden." *Bossier*, 528 U.S. at 359 (Souter, J., concurring in part and dissenting in part). It means to "curtail," rather than take away, the voting right. American Heritage Dictionary 4 (1969)." (Dissenting Opinion on Mark Brnovivh, Attorney General of Arizona, Et Al., Petitioners v. Democratic National Committee, Et Al. by Associate Justice Elena Kagan, 2021).

If a voter in Arizona appears at a polling place, that is not designated to them. They are not being a denied the vote. They are instructed by an election official, the right location to vote. I do not call that voter suppression; I call it a clear law of the standard of Arizona to assist in any way to the voter.

What I have a problem with this electoral standard of a law is that it is showing mixed procedures of voting. While the voter is registered to vote at their designated polling place. It is not a requirement for the voter to drop off their ballot at their designated polling place. The voter can drop off the ballot at any location, even if that voter is not registered in that district. I call this a discrepancy in the law of the standard and procedures of Arizona electoral law.

I can see where a voter of any income means, regardless of race, sex, or skin color works at a different location than where there polling place is located. That is not showing discriminatory intent to the voter.

If a voter wants to change the voting standard for vote-in-person. I would suggest that they contact their legislator and change or amend the law. To perform a judicial review on a state electoral law is not proper and constitutional. To present discriminatory intent on this case and on this law is arbitrary, capricious, and unconstitutional. Especially where there are no signs of discriminatory intent. And the no need for federal government enforcement to enforce the Fifteenth Amendment.

Let us discuss the main reason that the federal court is discussing this case. As much as I am disgusted that this nation had to endure a civil war for the unfortunate reason of maintaining a human rights violation. But also disgusted with what came after the war. The constant contradiction of several sovereign States against the federal constitution. Because of this contradiction and ignorance of some individuals, we had to endure a strong, rogue, and arrogant meddling federal government. There would be no potential voter discrimination across the board regarding of race or color if individuals in power would have abided to the constitution and learnt the rules of federalism.

The game may have changed the course but the rules remain intact to pursue a healthy form of representative American Republic of sovereign States.

"Even if state actors had purposely discriminated, they would likely be "ab[le] to offer a non-racial rationalization," supported by "a false trail" of "official resolutions" and "other legislative history eschewing any racial motive." *Id.*, at 37. So only a results-focused statute could prevent States from finding ways to abridge minority citizens' voting rights." (Dissenting Opinion on Mark Brnovivh, Attorney General of Arizona, Et Al., Petitioners v. Democratic National Committee, Et Al. by Associate Justice Elena Kagan, 2021).

"But when to conclude—looking to effects, not purposes—that a denial or abridgement has occurred? Again, answering that question is subsection (b)'s function. See, *supra*, at 12-13. It teaches that a violation is established when, "based on the totality of circumstances," a State's electoral system is "not equally open" if members of a racial group. And then the subsection tells us what that means. A system is not equally open if members of one race have "less opportunity" than others to cast votes, to participate in politics, or to elect representatives. The key demand, then, for equal political opportunity across races." (Dissenting Opinion on Mark Brnovivh, Attorney General of Arizona, Et Al., Petitioners v. Democratic National Committee, Et Al. by Associate Justice Elena Kagan, 2021).

"And that is so even if (as is usually true) the law does not single out any race, but instead is facially neutral. Suppose, as Justice Scalia once did, that a county has a law limiting "voter registration [to] only three hours a week." *Chisom*, 501 U.S., at 408 (dissenting opinion). And suppose that policy makes it "more difficult for blacks to register than white" –say, because the jobs African Americans disproportionately hold make it harder to take time off that window. Ibid. Those citizens, Justice Scalia concluded, would then "have less opportunity 'to participate in the political process' than whites, and Section 2 would therefore be violated." (Dissenting Opinion on Mark Brnovivh, Attorney General of Arizona, Et Al., Petitioners v. Democratic National Committee, Et Al. by Associate Justice Elena Kagan, 2021).

* * *

Let us take a short detour in discussing a case where Justice Kagan brings up and targets the late Justice Antonin Scalia on his dissent. The case in which she discusses that many sovereign States have found ways to disproportionate voters of a minority race was the one decided in 1990, *Chisom v. Roemer, Governor of Louisiana, Et Al.* My question to the esteemed state government of the Pelican state is why are they permitting to place judges on the ballot box? Judges do not have a sheer representation of the popular demand. They have no agenda or interests for public office, and therefore excluded to participate in state elections. That should have been my first response to this lawsuit and remanded this issue back to the state legislature for further legislative review to change their methods of judge positions from electing to appointing.

But here is the dilemma of an everyday problem in our American Republic ever since 1913. That we have created an illusion of populist democracy. Therefore, we have now concluded that these United States of America has become a form of populist democracy and there is an "illusive will" of the people to come first over the will of the sovereign State. The will of the people does play a role within our republic but in the form of representative republic, not in a populist democracy.

"Section 2 of the Voting Rights Act of 1965 is not some all-purpose weapon for well-intentioned judges to wield as they please in the battle against discrimination. It is a statute. I thought we had adopted a regular method for interpreting the meaning of the language in its textual context; and second, using established canons of construction, ask whether there is any clear indication that some permissible meaning other than the ordinary one applies. If not—and especially if a good reason for the ordinary meaning appears plain—we apply that ordinary meaning." (Dissenting Opinion on Chisom v. Roemer, Governor of Louisiana, Et Al. by Associate Justice Antonin Scalia, 1990).

Justice Scalia, a great jurist of the modern high court era, knows the law and the Constitution quite well. He acknowledges that the judicial process is not there to use a law and alter it to please their specific and special interest agendas. The current statute of the 1965 VRA means what it says and says what it means. If there is any hint of jurists attempting to behave like legislators. He will call them out and register his dissent. That is what he did with this dissent and rightly so.

"Today, however the Court adopts a method quite out of accord with that usual practice. It begins not with what the statute must mean absent particular phenomena ([W]e are convinced that if Congress had . . . an intent [to exclude judges] Congress would have made it explicit in the statute, or at least some of the Members would have identified or mentioned it at some point in the unusually extensive legislative history," ante, at 396 (emphasis added)); and the Court then interprets the words of the statute to fulfill its expectation." (Dissenting Opinion on Chisom v. Roemer, Governor of Louisiana, Et Al. by Associate Justice Antonin Scalia, 1990).

"Finding nothing in the legislative history affirming that judges were excluded from the coverage of Section 2, the Court gives the phrase "to elect representatives" the quite extraordinary meaning that covers the election of judges." (Dissenting Opinion on Chisom v. Roemer, Governor of Louisiana, Et Al. by Associate Justice Antonin Scalia, 1990).

This Court back in 1991 has once again made a mockery to the rules of federalism in pertaining to the electoral laws of each sovereign state. The issue that occurred in Louisiana was indeed a possibility of disproportionate of minority voters towards an election of judges. But this does not mean that federal jurisdiction needs to be reviewed and affirmed. There should not be any federal judicial review because the law clearly states it and should have been remanded back to the state's state legislature for review.

"Our job begins with a text that Congress has passed and the President has signed. We are to read the words of that text as any ordinary Member of Congress would have read them, see Holmes, The Theory of Legal Interpretation, 12 Harv. L. Rev. 417 (1899), and apply the meaning so determined. In my view, that reading reveals that Section 2 extends to vote dilution claims for the elections of representatives only, and judges are not representatives." (Dissenting Opinion on Chisom v. Roemer, Governor of Louisiana, Et Al. by Associate Justice Antonin Scalia, 1990).

There is ample reason that I admire former Associate Justice Antonin Scalia. A man of true judicial convictions and upholder to the clear letter of the Constitution.

The job of a person of the law is to deal to interpret the law as it is written by an act of congress or the individual state legislature. It was never the establishment of the judicial review process to create, amend or repeal any laws.

Judges have not been a popular representation unlike a legislator. Since judges are not representatives, and not dictated under the 1982 Amendments to the VRA, then this case should not have reached a federal judiciary review. The modern age of the Supreme Court has been wielding power away from the sovereign states and into claws of a national government. The decision of 1991 regarding this case brings an attack to the rules of federalism and the distinct difference in why the Fifteenth Amendment and the Voting Rights Act were passed and has no bearing to the 2021 Arizona decision. Both cases serve as a reminder to the federalism principle to state sovereignty and a guidance to the federal constitution.

In both cases, every single American citizen voted in an election if the election were for a representative or non-representative government. The Fifteenth Amendment gave a new opening for electoral judicial activism to recognize all citizens to vote in elections, fairly and equally. If there were any injustice at the voting booth and the evidence was clear, then the federal government has the right to intervene. This was a historical fact prior to 1965 and the national government had every right to intervene. But after 1965, the systematic discrimination at the polling place had decreased immensely. Now has entered a new era of potential discriminatory intent that has no basis under the Fifteenth Amendment or the 1965 Voting Rights Act. It is a new era of judicial jurisprudence in trying to prove any sign of discriminatory intent where there is none. It is the job of the highest court of the land to remand these cases in dispute back to the state's respective assembly.

"Though this text nowhere speaks of "vote dilution," Thornburg v. Gingles, 478 U.S. 30 (1986), understood it to proscribe practices which produce that result, identifying as the statutory basis for a dilution claim the second of the two phrases highlighted above—"to elect representatives of their choice." Under this interpretation, the other highlighted phrase—"to participate in the political process"— is left for other *nondilution* section 2 violations. If, for example, a county permitted voter registration for only three hours one day a week, and that made it more difficult for blacks to register than whites, blacks would have less opportunity "to participate in the political process" than whites, and Section 2 would therefore be violated—even if the number of potential black voters was so small that they would on no hypothesis be able to elect their own candidate, see Blumstein, Proving Race Discrimination, 69 Va. L. Rev. 633, 706-707 (1983)." (Dissenting Opinion on Chisom v. Roemer, Governor of Louisiana, Et Al. by Associate Justice Antonin Scalia, 1990).

* * *

The comparison that Justice Kagan did in her dissent in the 2021 Arizona electoral case has truly no bearing in this case where she added a comment from Justice Scalia in this 1991 Louisiana case. And here is my summation of her dissent towards Scalia's 1991 dissent.

"And that is so even if (as is usually true) the law does not single out any race, but instead is facially neutral. Suppose, as Justice Scalia once did, that a country has a law limiting "voter registration" [to] only three hours one a day a week." *Chisom*, 501 U.S., at 408 (dissenting opinion). And suppose that policy makes it "more difficult for blacks to register than whites"—say, because the jobs African Americans disproportionately hold make it harder to take time off in that window. *Ibid.* Those citizens, Justice Scalia concluded, would then "have less opportunity 'to participate in the political process' than whites, and

Section 2 would therefore be violated." (Dissenting Opinion on Mark Brnovivh, Attorney General of Arizona, Et Al., Petitioners v. Democratic National Committee, Et Al. by Associate Justice Elena Kagan, 2021).

Justice Kagan is a very smart and yet illusive and emotional Supreme Court Justice in inputting her own dissent by putting down other's dissent. For her to prove an unwise and unethical point to her opinion, she fails to write in concrete towards Scalia's dissent regarding the 1991 case and especially regarding this paragraph.

Justice Scalia stated that if "A county of a sovereign state creates a discrimination imbalance between blacks and whites with regarding polling hours, that would be a violation of Section 2". Scalia states the contradiction that many states, especially in the South were achieving prior to 1965 but that sealed their contradiction with the passage of Voting Rights Act.

Justice Kagan is trying to demonstrate emotions into her dissent, so she will obtain judicial and political sympathy. Then she will obtain proof or lack thereof of electoral discriminatory intent in these cases.

If the 1991 case was a potential black discrimination case involving African Americans in an election, in this case a judge's electoral election. The 1982 Amendments does not mention judges' elections to be anything as elections for representatives and therefore there is no need to apply federal judicial review.

"Congress also made plain, in calling for a totality-of-circumstances inquiry, that equal voting opportunity is a function of both law and background conditions—in other words, that a voting rule's validity depends on how the rule operates in conjunction with the facts on the ground. "[T]otality review," this Court has explained, stems from Congress's recognition of "the demonstrated ingenuity of state and local governments in hobbling minority voting power." *Johnson v. De Grandy*, 512 U.S. 997, 1018 (1994). Sometimes, of course, state actions overtly target a single race: For example, Congress was acutely aware in amending Section 2, of the elimination of polling places in African American neighborhoods. See S. Rep., at 10, 11 and n. 22; H. R. Rep at 17, 35. But sometimes government officials enact facially neutral laws that leverage—and become discriminatory by dint of –pre-existing social and economic conditions. The classic cases are literacy tests and poll taxes. A more modern example is the one Justice Scalia gave, of limited registration hours. Congress knew how those laws worked: It saw that "inferior education, poor employment opportunities, and low income"— all conditions often correlated with race—could turn even an ordinary seeming election rule into an effective barrier to minority voting in certain circumstances. *Thornburg v. Gingles*, 478 U.S. 30, 69 (1986) (plurality opinion)." (Dissenting Opinion on Mark Brnovivh, Attorney General of Arizona, Et Al., Petitioners v. Democratic National Committee, Et Al. by Associate Justice Elena Kagan, 2021).

Justice Kagan is stating an unfortunate, unconstitutional, and unprincipled past precedence in America's polling place electoral history. The violation of harsh and unconstitutional voter suppression laws upon voting citizens of a minority community ended in 1965.

Justice Scalia was simply pointing out that in present times, no state or local jurisdiction can propose such policies of shorter hours at the polling place. Especially, if those hours will be affected in polling locations of minority voters because that would be a violation of Section 2. I am simply retorting Justice Kagan's outlandish claim towards a former member of the high court that insinuates that person is standing with people wanting to deny the right of citizen's right to vote because of the color of their skin.

Justice Scalia follows the letter of the law. If the 1982 Amendments to Section 2 of the Voting Rights Act did not have inscribed as judges to be part of representative elections, then it is the job of Congress to dictate it, not the high court. And quite frankly, it is not the job of the national Congress but the Louisiana State Legislature to dictate it. I only wished Justice Scalia would have been alive today and still on the bench to confine and befriend with Justice Kagan as he did with Justice Ginsburg. To give her some guidance towards federalism, state sovereignty, and the Constitution.

* * *

Justice Kagan's portion in trying to discredit the late Justice Scalia's dissent on the 1982 Amendments and the Louisiana case, in plain terms, a slick attorney trick to gain some popularity among the masses. If the 1982 Amendments to the Voting Rights Act did not cover judicial elections, because judges are not representatives. Then this case should have been remanded back to Louisiana. It should have been sent to their state legislature review, not court review. Instead, we got a high court dictating unconstitutional policy, policy not dictated into the law and in our federal constitution. I did not buy that Justice Kagan was sincere and truthful and neither should the rest of the American citizenry.

Let's return to discuss the legislation in question from the sovereign state of Arizona that is trying to prove discriminatory intent. The reason we are behind this debacle and trying to make a case that there is no discriminatory intent against the sovereign citizens of Arizona. There is a complete respect and guidance to the federal constitution and its Fifteenth Amendment.

In the mid-2000s, the federal government in their infinite and unnatural wisdom of rogue and arrogance established a commission on electoral issues in trying to slither like a slippery snake of electoral regulation into the fifty sovereign states. From what I have seen from the national government agenda, there is nothing more arrogant from the general government of the United States are clearly trying to impose their control onto the states.

But ironically, Justice Kagan does not mention this commission in her dissent. But Justice Alito does and let us digest and expose this commission's report to further comprehend to what I have been detailing the rogue and arrogance of this general government.

But regarding the Arizona case and this case involving judge's elections in Louisiana, they really must prove discriminatory intent to involve the high court for judicial review. If there is discriminatory intent, then the Court must remand its findings to the state legislature of that sovereign State for review to amend or repeal. But it is not the job of the Courts, let alone the high court of the land to dictate electoral policy onto the sovereign states.

"Even if the plaintiffs had shown a disparate burden caused by HB 2023, the State's justifications would suffice to avoid Section 2 liability. "A State indisputably has a compelling interest in preserving the integrity of its election process." *Purcell v. Gonzalez*, 549 U.S. 1, 4 (2006) (*per curiam*) (internal quotations marks omitted). Limiting the classes of persons who may handle early ballots to those likely to have ulterior motives deters potential fraud and improves voter confidence." (Opinion Brief on Mark Brnovivh, Attorney General of Arizona, Et Al., Petitioners v. Democratic National Committee, Et Al. by Associate Justice Samuel Alito, 2021).

It is in the best interest of the sovereign state to acknowledge and maintain the federal Constitution's interest in obtaining electoral constitutional integrity. The federal Constitution's interest is to maintain that there is no discriminatory intent that damages the integrity of our American republic of sovereign states. The sovereign states are the key players in maintaining that integrity.

Sovereign states established a photographic ID card, giving equal access at the early ballot box or polling place is a sure way in keeping that integrity. In 2006, the high court saw no dangers of that integrity when Arizona citizens proposed an ID voting law in 2004. As now as then, I see no issues of discriminatory intent being committed within the boundaries of that sovereign state.

"That was the view of the bipartisan Commission on Federal Election reform chaired by former President Jimmy Carter and former Secretary of State James Baker. The Carter-Baker Commission noted that "[a] bsentee balloting is vulnerable to abuse in several ways:… Citizens who vote at home, at nursing homes, at the work place, or in church are more susceptible to pressure, overt and subtle, or to intimidation." Report of the Comm'n on Fed. Election Reform, Building Confidence in U.S. Elections 46 (Sept. 2005)." (Opinion Brief on Mark Brnovivh, Attorney General of Arizona, Et Al., Petitioners v. Democratic National Committee, Et Al. by Associate Justice Samuel Alito, 2021).

When creating legislative initiatives concerning vote-by-mail and absentee voting, we must consider the common-sense initiative of humanity instead of an initiative full of emotions.

"HB 2023 likewise passes muster under the results test of Section 2. Arizonans who receive early ballots can submit them by going to a mailbox, a post office, an early ballot drop box, or an authorized election official's office within the 27-day early voting period. They can also drop off their ballots at any polling place or voting center on election day, and in order to do so, they can skip the line of voters waiting to vote in person. 329 F. Supp. 3d, at 839 (citing ECF Doc. 361, Paragraph 57). Making any of these trips—much like traveling to an assigned polling place—falls squarely within the heartland of the "unusual burdens of voting." Crawford, 553 U.S., at 198 (opinion of Stevens, J.). And voters can also ask a statutorily authorized proxy—a family member, a household manager, or a caregiver—to mail a ballot or drop it off at any time within 27 days of an election." (Opinion Brief on Mark Brnovivh, Attorney General of Arizona, Et Al., Petitioners v. Democratic National Committee, Et Al. by Associate Justice Samuel Alito, 2021).

* * *

This form of educative electoral agency is nothing more than infiltrating and undermining the rightly state sovereign doctrine articles that states have received since 1787.

"While vote by mail appears to increase turnout for local elections, there is no evidence that it significantly expands participation in federal elections. Moreover, it raises concerns about privacy, as citizens voting at home may come under pressure to vote for certain candidates, and it increases the risk of fraud. Oregon appears to have avoided significant fraud in its vote-by-mail elections by introducing safeguards to protect ballot integrity, including signature verification. Vote by mail is, however, likely to increase the risks of fraud and of contested elections in other states, where the population is more mobile, where there is some history of troubled elections, or where the safeguards for ballot integrity are weaker. (Report of the Comm'n on Fed. Election Reform, Building Confidence in U.S. Elections 46 (Sept. 2005).

"The case of King County, Washington, is instructive. In the 2004 gubernatorial elections, when two in three ballots there were cast by mail, authorities lacked an effective system to track the number of ballots sent or returned. As a result, King County election officials were unable to account for all absentee ballots. Moreover, a number of provisional ballots were accepted without signature verification. The failures to account for all absentee ballots and to verify signatures on provisional ballots became issues in the protracted litigation that followed Washington state's 2004 gubernatorial election." (Report of the Comm'n on Fed. Election Reform, Building Confidence in U.S. Elections 46 (Sept. 2005).

My concern to this Arizona electoral law is not the idea of vote-by-mail as I see it. It is the constant contradiction of the legal perks of vote-by-mail and the vote-in-person. Arizona's HB2023 gives electoral leeway to the voter by sending off their ballot in many different forms. The issue I have is that when you give too much leeway to one form of voting but not to the other is a recipe for misleading and legal turmoil. In this vote-by-mail to what Arizona is offering to her citizens is wide range of sending off their ballots in different formats. While if you vote-in-person, you are required to go to the assigned specific location and if arrived at another polling place, you are being directed to the assigned one. If in person, you are being directed to your assigned voting location, why can't your ballot?

If the sovereign state of Oregon has created a system that shows no signs of corruption or discriminatory intent. Then other states should follow that example and apply a similar standard but under their own law and regulations. If Oregon requires a "signature verification" on their absentee ballot, and is a must, then there are no exemptions to the rule and voters are expected to follow that rule. That rule of federalism.

If there is a state government employee not following that rule and finds a way to commit a corrupt act or discriminatory intent. That government employee must be investigated, and if proved of their guilty changes, must be prosecuted, and sentenced. If in Washington State, they also required a signature verification on their ballots and some were not verified, then there is a state government employee taking the rule into their own hands and must be dealt properly in the due process system established in this republic.

It is the solemn duty of the sovereign state to regulate and enforce that election rule. It is not intended for the national government to regulate elections.

To handle acts of corruption and findings of discriminatory intent in elections are best handled by the sovereign state. It is the solemn duty of the sovereign state to regulate and enforce that election rule. It is not intended for the national government to regulate elections.

I see there is a problem with the electoral law of the sovereign state of Washington. Sovereign states can follow other states' models of electoral law if it is applied at their own legislative procedure. We cannot let the courts apply without legislative affirmation.

As we saw the debacle in Florida, 2000, and the constant harassment in 2020.

The Carter-Baker Electoral Commission Report was presented to the republic as a notice to all sovereign states to apply the Constitution as it is currently written into their laws. They are simply recommending to the sovereign states. When the federal government, whether it is the high court, national Congress, or the executive branch tries to recommend any actions to the states, it leads to further control of the sovereignty of the States. One of them is the strict assurance that their residents of their state are confined to vote without no hint of harassment or discrimination. After 1965, with the national congressional assistance to enforce the Fifteenth Amendment, sovereign states have been given strict instructions to comply. Till this day, we have not seen any more days of Jim Crow laws in southern and rocky mountain states.

From what I have read, this report is not stating, and hope does not state on other parts, the consideration of a national electoral law. This is something that I do hope it never comes to existence because that will *truly* be the end of our American Republic of sovereign States.

* * *

To this day, since 1965, a sovereign State has not denied the right to vote to a citizen. The Fifteenth Amendment has guaranteed that right since 1868. Then it was re-affirmed with the passage of the Voting

Rights Act (VRA) in 1965. What the VRA does not state or make claim of is that it does not grant the federal government to create and mandate a national standard of voting.

"So the State has no duty to substitute a non-discriminatory rule that would adequately serve its professed goal. Like the rest of today's opinion, the majority's treatment of the collection ban flouts what Section 2 commands: the eradication of election rules resulting in unequal opportunities for minority voters." (Dissenting Opinion on Mark Brnovivh, Attorney General of Arizona, Et Al., Petitioners v. Democratic National Committee, Et Al. by Associate Justice Elena Kagan, 2021).

Removing drop ballots boxes or directing voters to their proper polling place is not a new result of showing unequal opportunities to any such voter. This is not 1957 Alabama where poll taxes and literacy tests were a classic move of voter suppression and denying our basic Fifteenth Amendment right to vote. The Voting Rights Act of 1965 says it in its name. It is the Right to Vote Act, not the Counting Votes Act.

The Arizona electoral law in question has flaws that nobody dares to bring up. They are putting more ballot boxes in the streets but redistricting the polling places across the state. The voting standards and counting procedures should be equal at best and not so a disproportionate in showing access in one way and diminish access to the other. Then the progressive movement will take

> It is the Right to Vote Act, not the Counting Votes Act.

it at face value and start to rewrite the law and create disastrous court rulings into legislative policy.

"But Congress gets to make that call. Because it has not done so, this Court's duty is to apply the law as it is written. The law that confronted one of this country's most enduring wrongs; pledged to give every American, of every race, an equal chance to participate in our democracy; and now stands as the crucial tool to achieve that goal. That law, of all laws, deserves the sweep and power Congress gave it. That law, of all laws, should not be diminished by this Court." (Dissenting Opinion on Mark Brnovivh, Attorney General of Arizona, Et Al., Petitioners v. Democratic National Committee, Et Al. by Associate Justice Elena Kagan, 2021).

Indeed, that the national Congress made that call. They made it so that everybody has the right to vote and equal access to an individual ballot. And in 1965, they affirmed that directive. But the Congress did not affirm anything to have a national counting directive for all the sovereign states. And the Court is to interpret the law, nay to apply, establish or change.

If the Fifteenth Amendment becomes diminished by any governing body of the general government or individual sovereign rights, then the citizen has a right to complain, till then, no right to vote has been diminished.

"Arizona's out-of-precinct policy and HB 2023 do not violate Section 2 of the VRA, and HB2023 was not enacted with a racially discriminatory purpose. The judgement of the Court of Appeals is reversed, and the cases are remanded for further proceedings consistent with this opinion. It is so ordered." (Opinion Brief on Mark Brnovivh, Attorney General of Arizona, Et Al., Petitioners v. Democratic National Committee, Et Al. by Associate Justice Samuel Alito, 2021).

The sovereign states understand that after 1965, the right to vote should not be denied to all citizens of this republic. The Voting Rights Act shows affirmation of the Fifteenth Amendment that no vote shall be violated or prohibit to be casted. The votes are being casted, now comes that the voter should comprehend the standard and procedure of their state electoral laws.

As Justice Sandra Day O'Connor once stated in the 2000 case of *Bush v. Gore* towards the voter's participation in their right to vote.

"Why is not it the standard, the one that voters are instructed to follow, for goodness sake, I mean it could not be clearer. Why don't we go to that standard?" – Associate Justice Sandra Day O'Connor, *Bush v. Gore*, 2000.

The voters have a right to vote, and with that right to vote comes responsibility and understanding to follow it, to continue to obtain that right.

* * *

The Supreme Court now heard a case titled, "*Moore v. Harper*", (docket case # 21-1271) in which I believe is making a mockery of the state sovereign doctrine of the electoral clauses.

Let us pose the question of this case presented to the Court and see how you and I can debate it and prove if the sovereign States hold the power. And let us answer it while we review the transcripts of the oral arguments.

"Whether a State's judicial branch may nullify the regulations governing the "Manner of holding Elections for Senators and Representatives...prescribed...by the Legislature thereof," U.S. CONST. art 1; Section 4; clause 1, and replace them with regulations of the state courts' own devising, based on vague state constitutional provisions purportedly vesting the state judiciary with power to prescribe whatever rules it deems appropriate to ensure a "fair" or "free" election."

Does a state judicial branch have that power to nullify any regulations from a state legislative directive to govern the manner of holding elections for Senators and Representatives as a legislature prescribes and directs?

To place a direct and straight answer, it would happen to be a definite no. A state's judicial branch may "not" nullify, or even meddle in any state legislative directive with regarding electoral procedures and standards. Even if the electoral law may seem unconstitutional, it is up to the state legislature to act accordingly to place the safest piece of legislation for their people.

For the question to state that the state courts are here to dictate what rules are deemed appropriate to ensure a "fair" and "free" election, is a power that the Courts do not have and never had. The courts are not here to determine the rules. The courts are here to interpret these rules and if they deemed it unconstitutional.

Their job is to not strike a law, but advise the legislature thereof, to amend and/or repeal the rules. The executive of the State is there to execute the law, or veto the law, if the governor does not see fit that this law is constitutionally viable. (*Smiley v. Horn*, 1932).

And here we go on the ride to see who will dictate electoral standards for our republic. Here we go again, to see how the federal government and its progressive allies continue to undermine the electoral clauses.

The Fifteenth Amendment was established for all our citizens, the guaranteed right to vote. It is the right to present your ballot and it shall not be denied. What the Fifteenth Amendment does not say is that the federal government, the right to impose national electoral and counting standards. The 1965 Voting Rights Act affirmed the guaranteed right to vote, it does not affirm a counting standard. That counting standard is being left to the sovereign States to regulate and enforce. It is that quite simple, and we all know why the general government wants to bypass the states' authority, it is all about control.

When I state that the power is reserved to the sovereign States, it is clearly meant the state legislature. The state legislature is the directive's voice of the people.

"Were they exclusively under the control of the state governments, the general government might be easily dissolved. But if they be regulated properly by the state legislatures, the congressional control will very probably never be exercised." (The Debates in the Several States Conventions, vol. 3, James Madison).

James Madison, the father of our principled document, always standing true to its federalism principles. If state governments play by the constitutional rules and respect its citizen residents and their neighboring sovereign states. Then there would never be meddling from the national government. We the states do not need meddling from the federal government in establishing national directives or the federal courts dictating uninterpreted legislation onto the states.

Only a few jurists of the court have interpreted the constitution author's words onto theirs and kept it in the original format as presented to the convention in 1787.

The late Associate Justice to the high court, Justice Antonin Scalia truly was the sole jurist that spoke the wordings of the Constitution as they have written it. He made no mistakes in expressing his original intent views and never presented the principled document as a "living-Original" document. The Constitution is an original document residing in a world of today living up to its principled standards. The electoral clauses in the Constitution resides in the power of the States and not the national government.

"It seems to me utterly implausible that the Framers wanted federal courts limited to traditional judicial cases only when they were pronouncing upon the rights of Congress and the President, and not when they were treading upon the powers of state legislatures and executives. Quite to the contrary, I think they would be *all the more averse* to unprecedented judicial meddling by federal courts with the branches of their state governments." (Dissenting Opinion of Arizona State Legislature v. Arizona Independent Redistricting Commission, by Associate Justice Antonin Scalia, 2015).

Justice Scalia knew what court cases and legislation belongs in the hands of the federal government and the sovereign states. Electoral laws and standards, from national presidential elections to statewide elections belongs in the hands of the state legislatures. The federal government granted this right for all sovereign States to give their citizens, the right to vote. But the federal government was not granted the right, nor the power to control the electoral counting and standards of each state's elections.

"Normally, having arrived at that conclusion, I would express no opinion on the merits unless my vote was necessary to enable the court to product a judgment. In the present case, however, the majority's resolution of merits question ("legislature means "the people") is so outrageously wrong, so utterly devoid of textual or historic support, so flatly in contradiction of prior Supreme Court cases, so obviously the willful product of hostility to districting by state legislatures, that I cannot adding my vote to the devastating dissent of the Chief Justice." (Dissenting Opinion of Arizona State Legislature v. Arizona Independent Redistricting Commission, by Associate Justice Antonin Scalia, 2015).

Districting and re-districting of electoral areas in a sovereign State belongs in the realm of law to the sovereign State. The state legislature is not denying that person's right to vote, just because they re-district that voting location. It is a standard of electoral law and that still resides under Constitutional Article II.

Are the progressives of today's court trying to undermine Article II by establishing national electoral directives? I did not want the Florida supreme court to establish counting standards and procedures from the state of Texas onto Florida and would not have even liked for the Supreme Court to accept that precedent. If the high court would have accepted that unconstitutional precedent, then Donald J. Trump would have been unfortunately reelected, and it would have been the end of our representative republic.

"Second, after the Constitution was ratified, states kept regulating it. States like Delaware and Maryland and Mississippi expressly regulated federal elections, as did three quarters of the states." (Oral Argument of Mr. Neal K. Katyal, on behalf of the respondents on Moore v. Harper, December 7, 2022).

One thing is to deny a constitutional right to vote, and the other is to regulate elections. A state can continue to regulate elections without infringing on that constitutional right to vote. In all the electoral standards and laws that came after Bush v. Gore, 2000, I truly see no voter rights infringement of the citizens' Fifteenth Amendment voting right.

The respondents and today's left-wing progressives and right-wing nationalists truly have no idea how this nation was established. This nation should not be seeking to establish a national electoral standard from the left or the right. And we cannot let our courts create that standard. We cannot let our courts dictate one sovereign state standard to be imposed onto another state. As we cannot let our national Congress dictate a national electoral standard against the sovereignty of our States.

"There is certainly something legislative there, but I think that the overall point of *Smiley* is to say – and my friend says this is in the reply brief at page 6 – you take legislatures as you find them. He agrees with that proposition. That's what *Smiley* did as well. The legislature as it found – as it was found in Minnesota in *Smiley* was – ..." (Oral Argument of Mr. Neal K. Katyal, on behalf of the respondents on Moore v. Harper, December 7, 2022).

"And nobody here thinks the North Carolina Supreme Court is exercising a legislative function. We all agree on that too, right?" (Oral Question of Associate Justice Neil Gorsuch on Moore v. Harper, December 7, 2022).

"I am saying is that *Smiley* focused on two things, the word "legislature" but also the word "regulate. And together they create a law-making system, one of which was judicial review, well-established at the founding, far more established than the veto. So far more established than the veto. And so, you know, seven different states had judicial review at the founding. If the method of *Smiley* – the method of *Smiley* is to say, look, the founders know about the veto because it was in two states, did they textually exclude it in the language? The answer was no." (Oral Argument of Mr. Neal K. Katyal, on behalf of the respondents on Moore v. Harper, December 7, 2022).

The actual precedent of *Smiley* is not to give judicial precedence for the court to behave like a state legislature. The court detailed the word "legislature" because it is the legislature of the State that dictates the law, in this case, electoral law. The Court mentions the word "regulate" because it is the executive (governor) to foresee for regulating and enforcing of the law. Smiley decision mentions the two out of three branches of government that are in complete charge of overseeing the laws being created and enforced. What the respondents are trying to install is an imaginary claim of "judicial 'legislative' review". It is not judicial review of the courts examining and interpreting the law. They are finally wanting the courts to create the laws of the States and take it away from the people's representation.

"Mr. Katyal, can I ask you some questions about the boundaries of your argument. So suppose a state constitution says that congressional districts will be determined by the state supreme court exercising legislative power. Is that consistent with the Elections Clause?" (Oral Question of Associate Justice Samuel Alito on Moore v. Harper, December 7, 2022).

"We don't think it would be, Your Honor. So we think, in general, there may be some redefinition of the legislature that Arizonians – the Arizona decision might permit. That isn't what we are arguing here. We're talking about ordinary checks and balances like judicial review." (Oral Argument of Mr. Neal K. Katyal, on behalf of the respondents on Moore v. Harper, December 7, 2022).

"All right, Suppose that the state constitution says that the legislature can adopt congressional maps, but in that instance, the state supreme court shall sit as a council of revision to determine whether the maps are fair." <small>(Oral Question of Associate Justice Samuel Alito on Moore v. Harper,</small>

<small>December 7, 2022).</small>

"We do think that the history there would suggest it is. Nothing in our argument, of course, depends on it. Again, ordinary judicial review, that is all we think you should reach in this case. Not that, but the New York example is exactly that." <small>(Oral Argument of Mr. Neal K. Katyal, on behalf of the respondents on Moore v. Harper, December 7, 2022).</small>

"Well, that's not really judicial review. That is because they're not reviewing it for anything." <small>(Oral Question of Associate Justice Samuel Alito on Moore v. Harper, December 7, 2022).</small>

"Nothing in our position depends on it, Your Honor, but the historical test, which is what he's using, New York in 1792, did exactly that." <small>(Oral Argument of Mr. Neal K. Katyal, on behalf of the respondents on Moore v. Harper, December 7, 2022).</small>

"The state constitution – the state supreme court says that the essence of our state constitution is fairness. It doesn't point to a particular provision in the state constitution. It just says the essence of our state constitution is fairness to all of our citizens, and the map adopted by the legislature is not fair." <small>(Oral Question of Associate Justice Samuel Alito on Moore v. Harper, December 7, 2022).</small>

"Yes, Your Honor, we think that would – again, nothing turns on that here, but the answer to your question is yes, we think that would be constitutional, and the reason why is because there's a trident of safeguards that would prevent any sort of abuse. The first one, the safeguard, is in the state process itself. As Judge Sutton's work explains, state courts have all sorts of mechanisms to restrain them, including popular accountability and, as Justice Barrett pointed out a moment ago, a much easier amendment process." (Oral Argument of Mr. Neal K. Katyal, on behalf of the respondents on Moore v. Harper, December 7, 2022).

If there is any abuse orchestrated by a state legislature. It is the responsibility of the citizen to take command and elect a new representation. Judge Sutton is quite wrong in one thing in describing the work of the state courts. They do have the mechanisms, but to not restrain them, but to interpret and send back the law in question for review or repeal.

"Second, the founders laced into the Elections Clause itself a specific remedy for your concern, which is that Congress can come in and supplant – any particular state court decision they don't like, they can say this North Carolina map should be reinstated, they could supplant all the state constitutions." (Oral Argument of Mr. Neal K. Katyal, on behalf of the respondents on Moore v. Harper, December 7, 2022).

"But can't you say the same thing about allowing the legislature to do – which is popularly elected, to do the – to make the map? Congress can always come in." (Oral Question of Associate Justice Samuel Alito on Moore v. Harper, December 7, 2022).

"They said that's just indicia of the fact that the founders distrusted state legislatures and wanted checks and balances. Here, of course, we're only seeking ordinary ones." (Oral Argument of Mr. Neal K. Katyal, on behalf of the respondents on Moore v. Harper, December 7, 2022).

"Were they exclusively under the control of the state governments, the general government might be easily dissolved. But if they be regulated properly by the state legislatures, the congressional control will very probably never be exercised." (The Debates in the Several States Conventions, vol. 3, James Madison).

It is not that the framers distrusted state legislatures. They granted them power to act responsibly in creating laws for their citizens. Laws to be regulated properly and constitutionally. If the framers were to have been distrustful of them, then they would have made the Constitution to be in absolute control by the federal government. That clearly was never their intention.

James Madison, the father of the Constitution, the man who wrote the principled document. He never intended to give too much power to the federal government as to create the same government, they all signed an independence charter in 1776.

This case that will shake our individual and sovereign States' electoral clauses rights. It will change the course of our independence of our state legislatures came to a horrible decision on June 27, 2023.

The high court decided to grant judicial 'legislative' review on all electoral cases across this union of sovereign States. They are completely undermining Article I or Article II so to give the federal government the ultimate complete and control of all 50 state standards into one national voting standard.

The high court does not blatantly deny this right that the states have also under the Tenth Amendment.

"The Elections Clause of the Federal Constitution requires "the Legislature" of each State to prescribe the rules governing federal elections. Art. I, Section 4, cl. 4." (Judgment syllabus of Moore v. Harper, 2023).

"This Court has jurisdiction to review the judgement of the North Carolina Supreme Court in Harper I that adjudicated the Federal Elections Clause." (Judgment syllabus of Moore v. Harper, 2023).

"Although the Elections Clause does not exempt state legislatures from their ordinary constraints imposed by state law, federal courts must not abandon their duty to exercise judicial review. This Court has an obligation to ensure that state court interpretations of state law do not evade federal law. For example, States "may not sidestep" the Takings Clause by disavowing traditional property interests." (Judgment syllabus of Moore v. Harper, 2023).

The elections clause is a right guaranteed to the States and mandated by its Tenth Amendment. Early Americans and today's progressives were trying to undermine this sovereign state power and have totally misunderstood the philosophy of judicial review. If by judicial review, you mean that a court will examine a state law and dictate if that law should be remanded back to its state legislature for review. Then yes, it would be in a more perfect union republic to send it back to that state for review, amending, or repeal. When a state law happens to contradict the federal constitution, then in my opinion, it is when the Court to strike it down. For example, the apprenticeship and segregation laws passed in the mid-1860's to the early on of the Twentieth century.

The court is there for judicial review of a law, not for judicial 'legislative' review of a law. The court is not an elected body of men to act as legislators. Ever since the unprincipled decision of *Marbury v. Madison*, 1803. The people have seen the judicial system into a different light of governmental process. Especially how this republic was established to let the sovereign states be independent, fair, and free to govern themselves if they do not violate their citizen's rights. If this republic were perfect then we would not have the problems we have today, and therefore the preamble states, "a more perfect union" of sovereign States.

To insinuate that States, sidestep the constitution on electoral matters is an arrogant statement from the national government's high court. Yes, states have had past horrible experiences of sidestepping and trampling on individual's Ninth Amendment rights. But there will be no need for sidestepping on the election clauses of Article I and Article II. That is a right guaranteed by its own Tenth Amendment. It is the federal government that should not sidestep the powers and rights of the individuals and the States regarding these clauses. But unfortunately, we have a national government, from past and present executive administrations, high court, and Congress sidestepping these rights out of existence.

We do not need a clear definition of the elections clause but in the interest of sanity and clarity, I will point it out. For the interest of this American republic of sovereign States.

"The Elections Clause provides: "The Times, Places and Manner of holding Elections for Senators and Representatives, shall be prescribed in each State by the Legislature thereof; but the Congress may at any time by Law make or alter such Regulations, except as to the Places of chusing Senators." *Ibid*. The Clause "imposes" on state legislatures the "duty" to prescribe rules governing federal elections." (Opinion of the Court for Moore v. Harper, 2023 by Chief Justice John Roberts).

"It also guards "against the possibility that a State would refuse to provide for the election of representatives" by authorizing Congress to prescribe its own rules. Ibid." (Opinion of the Court for Moore v. Harper, 2023 by Chief Justice John Roberts).

"Their position rests on three premises, from which the conclusion follows." Dissenting Opinion of the Court for Moore v. Harper, 2023 by Associate Justice Clarence Thomas).

"The first premise is that "the people of a single State" lack any ability to limit powers "given by the people of the United States" as a whole. *McCollough v. Maryland*, 4 Wheat. 316, 429 (1819). This idea should be uncontroversial, as it is "the unavoidable consequence of th[e] supremacy" of the Federal Constitution and laws. Id., at 436. As the Court once put it (in a case about Article V ratifying power of state legislatures), "a federal function derived from the Federal Constitution… transcends any limitations sought to be imposed by the people of the State." *Leser v. Garnett*, 258 U.S. 130, 137 (1922)."

"The second premise is that regulating the times, places, and manner of congressional elections ""is no original prerogative of state power,'" so that "such power 'had to be delegated to, rather than reserved by, the States.'" This premise is firmly supported by this Court's precedents, which have also held that the Elections Clause is "the exclusive delegation of" such power, as "[n]o other constitutional provision gives the States authority over congressional elections."

"The third premise is that "the Legislature thereof" does not mean the people of the State or the State as an undifferentiated body politic, but rather, the lawmaking power as it exists under the State Constitution. This premise comports with the usual constitutional meanings of the words "State" and "Legislature," as well as this Court's precedence. A "state, and the legislature of a state, are quite different political beings." Story Section 628. "A state, in the ordinary sense of the Constitution, is a political community of free citizens...organized under a government sanctioned and limited by a written Constitution." Texas v. White, 7 Wall. 700, 721 (1869)." "'Legislature,'" on the other hand, generally means "'the representative body which ma[kes] the laws of the people. [T]he word 'Legislature' as used in the [the Elections Clause] means the lawmaking body or power of the state, as established by the State Constitution," or, put differently, "that body of persons within a state clothed with authority to make laws." Dissenting Opinion of the Court for Moore v. Harper, 2023 by Associate Justice Clarence Thomas).

Justice Thomas made a more justifiable case that the power of regulating a State's electoral standards and procedures reside in the hands of the individual sovereign State.

The first premise that Justice Thomas states that the idea in which the people have the power in these clauses is an illusion for the popular masses. The most destructive high court ruling in the early part of the nineteenth century made shot down any part of individual "We the People" power. Justice Thomas begins to lay down the true meaning of the states' electoral clauses.

It is a shame that the high court voted the way they did to undermine the election clauses and give power to this foolish theory of judicial review.

The second and third premises that JUSTICE THOMAS points out is quite clear that he states that the power is vested in the state legislature. Even though, the power of the vote of the people control the state legislatures' representation. It is the state legislature, thereof that controls to make the laws.

If the people who elect their representation do not like a law passed by the legislature, thereof, then it is up to the people to remind their representation to review a law that does not sit well with their constituent base.

If the courts get involve to "judicial review" a state or federal law, then let it be reviewed and remanded back to that state legislature for amending or repeal.

That to me is the accurate definition of judicial review. The court is set to review the legislation for their opinion. But they are not there to rewrite or repeal a law based on this judicial review. To get the legislator's attention, for them to change a law, it comes from their constituents…and it is called elections.

The power of Congress is not to set the electoral standards for all fifty states. It is to administer that all states play within the rules within their own sovereign State border. People have underestimated the power of the national government. They think that just because certain clauses state the word "regulate". They have been taught that it means that Congress has the power to enforce certain aspects of the Constitution. They could not be more incorrect and untruthful. Since before the 1787 Constitution to be adopted, Congress never had any regulatory power and to be honest, they still do not have that power. And when it comes to regulatory power of Article I or Article II, they do not enjoy that enforcement power.

If a sovereign State refuses to send their congressional delegation to the national Congress, then it is the problem of that affected state, not the entire republic. As I stated in my second book, *The Road to Liberty: Bringing an End to the 16th and 17th Amendments*, does Congress really have the power to prescribe electoral rules to set national electoral standards for all states? The answer is a straight and factful, NO.

One may even question the Act of 1866, forcing the States to bring their delegation all at that the same time for national representation is forcefully unconstitutional. This was done right after the southern states were re-admitted back into the union and to avoid any more insurrectionists, then the radical republicans in a majority Congress made a national law for electoral standards and procedures.

Once the national government regained control of the rebellious southern states. They were no need for full centralized form of government. The issue of slavery had been resolved and made into a federal act of Congress, but the remaining aspects of state sovereignty and independence returned to their respective States. This Act of 1866 was not act of necessary and proper act and should have deemed unconstitutional by the high court for infringing upon Article I and Article II and under the Tenth Amendment.

But here we are where the national government have been undermining the state sovereign electoral rights since 1866 to the present.

"Shortly after the new maps became law, several groups of plaintiffs—including the North Carolina League of Conservation Voters, Common Cause, and individual voters—sued in state court." (Opinion of the Court for Moore v. Harper, 2023 by Chief Justice John Roberts).

"But "federal courts" cannot give answers simply because someone asks." Uzuegbunam, 592 U.S., at ____ (ROBERTS, C.J., dissenting) (slip op., at 12)" (Dissenting Opinion of the Court for Moore v. Harper, 2023 by Associate Justice Clarence Thomas).

The way to phrase this statement is that "federal courts are not here to be the solution to all our problems, just because someone is seeking answers." The federal government is not the solution to our problems, the federal government is the problem and continues to be that problem. But the sad thing is that we continue to make it a problem whether if now Trump was president or Biden is the current president.

"The State Supreme Court also rejected that the Elections Clause in the Federal Constitution vests exclusive and independent authority in state legislatures to draw congressional maps." (Opinion of the Court for Moore v. Harper, 2023 by Chief Justice John Roberts).

Justice Thomas most distinctly points out the exact third branches of government, federal and state.

"A Governor's *motives* for vetoing a certain bill are irrelevant to the effect to the effect of the veto as part of the legislative process, just as the motives that may lead one house of the legislature to reject a bill passed by the other house are irrelevant to the effect of its doing so. Put simply, when this power is conferred on the Governor of a State, it "makes him in effect a third branch *of the legislature.*" (Dissenting Opinion of the Court for Moore v. Harper, 2023 by Associate Justice Clarence Thomas).

This is what happens when individual citizens act with an emotional mind rather than with a just mind. Thanks to the awful decision in 1803, American citizens believe that they can take every single act of a state legislature to court. Not all laws are deemed to enter the halls of the high court especially when it has no constitutional backing.

Drawing congressional maps, executing voting standards and procedures are all legal processes set by Article I, II and under its Tenth Amendment doctrine. People have this impression that most of the state legislatures draw these congressional maps to oust or make it difficult for minority voters. There has never been found any truthful and factful evidence to that effect. You need to find discriminatory intent which no entity fighting against Article I and II has yet to discover to be factual, let alone truthful.

"JUSTICE THOMAS sees it differently. He correctly observes that the North Carolina Supreme Court has now dismissed the plaintiffs' claims with prejudice." (Opinion of the Court for Moore v. Harper, 2023 by Chief Justice John Roberts).

The majority of the Court chose the path of judicial 'legislative' review than an actual path of judicial review. They in the end were completely blindsided and lost to the principles of federalism. Justice Kavanaugh is certainly one justice in today's court that I hold no respect or regard to his constitutional standards and state sovereign doctrine.

The Bush v. Palm Beach County Canvassing Bd., 531 U.S. 70, 76-78(2000) showed a clear way that state court cannot have that responsibility of judicial review when they are creating its own voting standard methods. The Florida Supreme Court took it upon themselves to change the law and disavow legally counted "punched-through" ballots to accept illegal "dimpled chad" and "hanging chad" ballots and even extend to a hand recount that was never a part of the Florida voting standard at that time.

"Federal Court review of a state court's interpretation of state law in a federal election case "does not imply a disrespect for state *courts* but rather a respect for the constitutionally prescribed role of state *legislatures*." Bush v. Gore, 531 U.S. 98, 115 (2000)

(Rehnquist, C.J., concurring)." (Concurring Opinion of the Court for Moore v. Harper, 2023 by Associate Justice Brett Kavanaugh).

The federal high court in the Florida 2000 case disrespected the role of the state *court* while respected the role of the state *legislatures*. And it was done rightly and justly so. That state *court* was not applying judicial review but judicial 'legislative' review.

This North Carolina case was quite the same as what happened in Florida, with the exception that one happened in an election and the other was preparing its voting standards and procedures for the next election.

But both state *courts* were not applying to interpret the law, they were applying to change the law. And by doing that, they were disrespecting the role of the state *legislatures*.

For federal court to step in and must apply so-called judicial review on a state court's decision or state legislature's law, is beyond tyrannical and arrogant. But they learned from their Master of the Court, Chief Justice John Marshall.

Both cases were a disregard to the rules of federalism and to the doctrine of state sovereignty and independence that helped establish this republic union of States. But, unfortunately and sadly, no one mentions these principled words to help bring back sanity and normalcy to our ailing republic.

"Chief Justice Rehnquist's standard is straightforward: whether the state court: "impermissibly distorted" state law "beyond what a fair reading required." Ibid. As I understand it, Justice Souter's standard, at least the critical language, is similar: whether the state court exceeded "the limits of reasonable" interpretation of state law. Id., at 133 (dissenting opinion). And the Solicitor General here has proposed another similar approach: whether the state court reached a "truly aberrant" interpretation of state law. Brief for United States as Amicus Curiae 27. As I see it, all three standards convey essentially the same point: Federal court review of a state court's interpretation of state law should be deferential, but deference is not abdication." (Concurring Opinion of the Court for Moore v. Harper, 2023 by Associate Justice Brett Kavanaugh).

State electoral law should always be deferential and above any federal order, but deference is not tyrannical.

> "Our consideration is limited to the
> present circumstances, for the problem
> of equal protection in election processes
> generally presents many complexities."
>
> (Per Curiam of Bush v. Gore, 2000).

When it comes to the electoral clauses of the constitution. These are guaranteed powers to the States without infringing on the right of the voter.

All three standards spoke volumes regarding a state court's interpretation on a voter standard and procedure law. But there was a reason that this federal court did not apply judicial review on the Florida 2000 case because judicial review does not apply on the Election clauses. The decision of the *Bush v.*

Gore case presents a clear case of independent state legislative theory, and it should be applied to all.

How the Florida State Supreme Court should have handled it is to have asked the Governor of the State of Florida to call for an emergency special legislative session to review the current voting standards and reviewed if dimple and/or hanging chad would be allowed to be counted. That is appropriate role of the state *legislature*, not the state *court*.

That statement above from *Bush v. Gore*, 2000, needs to be applied to protect the election clauses and the role of state *legislatures*. Those complexities must be relied with careful judgment on the state powers of Article I and Article II without the influence or coercion of judicial 'legislative' review from federal court and now added state court.

That statement speaks bigger volumes to what Justice Kavanaugh quoted from C.J. Rehnquist on his concurring opinion. I am not surprised that Justice Kavanaugh and the federal high court refuses to give the appropriate role of the state legislatures and grant full power and control to the national government's high court.

If we continue to allow the General Government of the United States to undermine and disavow of federalism and its state sovereign doctrine. We will be moved further from a union of sovereign States to a union of dependent States.

"State courts retain the authority to apply state constitutional restraints when legislatures act under the power conferred upon them by the Elections Clause.

But federal courts must not abandon their duty to exercise judicial review. In interpreting state law in this area, state courts may not exceed the bounds of ordinary judicial review as to unconstitutionally intrude upon the role specifically reserved to state legislatures by Article I, Section 4, of the Federal Constitution. Because we need not decide whether that occurred in today's case, the judgment of the North Carolina Supreme Court is affirmed." (Opinion of the Court for Moore v. Harper, 2023 by Chief Justice John Roberts).

Judicial Review has been completely taken out of a context from its original interpretation in 1803 to the present. A court gives an opinion on the law in question, but the opinion is only valid when its properly constitutionally adopted. I will give you the times the opinion has been constitutionally adopted; 1917 *Buchanan v. Wharley*; 1954 *Brown v. Board of Education;* 1967 *Loving v. Virginia*; 1989 *City of Richmond v. J.A. Croson*, 2020 *Kansas v. Garcia*, 2022 *Dobbs v. Jackson Women's Health Organization*. To just name a few, where the opinions of the court's judicial review is justified in my book. These laws were found to be constitutionally acceptable by the court, regardless if people do not agree.

The high court has a say in this process to establish a law to be constitutional or not. What they do not have is to introduce judicial 'legislative' review. They do not have a right to re-write, or repeal the law.

At these other times it is just an opinion and holds no constitutional accordance. These opinions must be remanded back to the state legislatures for further review, amending, or repeal.

Regarding judicial review, whether by the state court or high court on matters of the election clauses. In my opinion, this opinion in particular has no constitutional backing, and it should be considered to be an opinion only to be remanded back to the state legislature. The elections clauses' power is stated quite clear and there is no debate about it. The state has this power and guaranteed under its Tenth Amendment doctrine. But the voter must have common-sense knowledgeability of their state's voting standards.

"With those additional comments, I agree with the Court's conclusions that (i) state laws governing federal elections are subject to ordinary state court review, and (ii) a state court's interpretation of state law in a case implicating the Elections Clause is in turn subject to federal court review." (Concurring Opinion of the Court for Moore v. Harper, 2023 by Associate Justice Brett Kavanaugh).

"In most cases, it seems likely that the "the bounds of ordinary judicial review" will be a forgiving standard in practice, and this federalization of state constitutions will serve mainly to swell federal-court dockets with state constitutional questions to be quickly resolved with generic statements of deference to the state courts. They will arise happily hazardly, in the midst of quickly evolving, politically charged controversies, and the winners of federal elections may be decided by a federal court's expedited judgment that a state court exceeded "the bounds of ordinary judicial review" in construing the state constitution."

(Dissenting Opinion of the Court for Moore v. Harper, 2023 by Associate Justice Clarence Thomas).

I quite agree with Justice Thomas on his ending dissenting paragraph. This ruling serves as not only an attack on the rules of federalism and its state sovereign doctrine. But a beginning to nationalize for a centralized voting standard.

We have seen it in 2020 in where the right-wing Trumper nationalist movement wanted the high court to disavow the electoral codes of Pennsylvania, Wisconsin, and Georgia. And we have seen the left-wing progressive movement wanted the national Congress to establish a national voting standard act for all fifty sovereign States.

I fear that we are moving more quickly away from our founding principles and more into a centralized autocracy. The very same centralized autocracy that we fought back in 1776. I also fear that it does not matter if you are in today's America of Republicans, or Democrats; liberals, or conservatives, they are all trying to seek the same…more indoctrination of federalization policies into our independent and sovereign American states. This includes federalization of our individual and independent sovereign State elections.

The very idea of electoral federalization should be dismissed, refused, and nullified at the individual and state level against this intrusive federal government. I hope and the people and states acknowledge this intrusion and step away from their partisanship and return to the simple constitutional findings and principles. We must one day return to a true American republic of independent and sovereign States, united under the 1787 federal constitution. A federal constitution guaranteeing our rights away from a national and federal government.

* * *

In past cases, the Supreme Court made statements that we are seeing a federalization of electoral standards and procedures. A federalization of a central standards against the sovereign States.

From the federal executive branch to the national Congress, to the high court of the land, there has been constant undermining of our state's power in the electoral clauses. The power is quite clear and there should be no clear obstruction of this power to the states.

Before the passage of the 1965 Voting Rights Act, there was at large and clear discriminatory intent towards the minority citizens of this republic. There was poll taxes and literacy tests performed and quite frankly that would be stricken as unconstitutional.

Due to the passage of this act, the end of discriminatory intent was over. There was one thing that people need to be clear about this situation. The Voting Rights Act does not specify the abolishment of Article I and Article II. Those articles have remained in place to safeguard the rights and powers of the state legislature of each state.

"The Constitution entrusts state legislatures with the primary responsibility for drawing congressional districts, and legislative redistricting is an inescapably political enterprise." (Syllabus of Alexander, President of the South Carolina Senate v. South Carolina State Conference of the NAACP, 2024).

The Constitution entrusts the state legislatures for more than just drawing congressional districts. This document entrusts the state legislatures with handling the electoral procedures and standards of their state, and that includes drawing congressional districts. The only thing that state legislatures are forbidden to do is to set times and dates for elections, that is the duty of Congress.

"Drawing political districts is a task for politicians, not federal judges." (Concurring Opinion by Associate Justice C. Thomas for Alexander, President of the South Carolina Senate v. South Carolina State Conference of the NAACP, 2024).

"Determining the proper shape of a district is a political question not suited to resolution by federal courts." (Concurring Opinion by Associate Justice C. Thomas for Alexander, President of the South Carolina Senate v. South Carolina State Conference of the NAACP, 2024).

I may have had plenty of disagreements with Justice Thomas, but I do have to say that I quite agree with him by this statement. If you want to be more technical about it. The drawing of the electoral standards is the task for legislators, not federal judges or federal or state bureaucrats.

It is a political question best suited to be discussed, debated, resolved at the state legislative level.

"As a result, racial gerrymandering and vote dilution claims brought under the Fourteenth and Fifteenth Amendments are nonjusticiable." (Concurring

Opinion by Associate Justice C. Thomas for Alexander, President of the South Carolina Senate v. South Carolina State Conference of the NAACP, 2024).

Determining how a legislature would have drawn district lines in a vacuum is a fool's errand." (Concurring Opinion by Associate Justice C. Thomas for Alexander, President of the South Carolina Senate v. South Carolina State Conference of the NAACP, 2024).

"The State contends that its mapmakers looked exclusively at data from the last election and targeted people who had voted Democratic. If that was true, the State's actions (however unsavory and undemocratic) are immune from federal constitutional challenge. The challengers, though, offer a different account. They say that the mapmakers, not content with what the election data revealed, also reviewed and heavily relied on racial data—thus exploiting the well-known correlation between race and voting behavior. And if that is true, the challengers have a good constitutional claim, because the Equal Protection Clause forbids basing election districts mainly on race in order to achieve partisan aims." (Dissenting Opinion by Associate Justice E. Kagan for Alexander, President of the South Carolina Senate v. South Carolina State Conference of the NAACP, 2024).

Nowadays, state legislatures must be careful in how they draw up voting districts, especially in southern state legislatures. Because how many southern state legislatures abused their power in really suppressing minority citizen voters in the past, everybody now looks with a careful eye to avoid discriminatory voter intent. Quite frankly, I see no truth in the challenger's claim.

Let me put this scenario for all Americans, if the Oregon state legislature decides to re-draw their voting districts maps and split one conservative district into two districts. Would you consider that a violation of the Equal Protection Clause?

I would not. The reason behind is Article I, Section IV, Cl., 1 and Article II, Section I, Cl., II. What Oregon does with their electoral districts, is no different than South Carolina, and they are basing it under their own state's constitutional rights.

Let us continue to read Kagan's dissent and prove to the rest of the republic and my reader that this is not a violation of the Equal Protection Clause.

"The state officials repeatedly denied using race in choosing the people kicked out of District 1, insisting that they based their decisions on political data alone." (Dissenting Opinion by Associate Justice E. Kagan for Alexander, President of the South Carolina Senate v. South Carolina State Conference of the NAACP, 2024).

"Yet there is worse: The majority cannot begin to justify its ruling on the facts without in two ways reworking the law—each to impede racial gerrymandering cases generally. First, the majority though ostensibly using the clear error standard, effectively inverts it whenever a trial court rules against a redistricting state. Second, the majority invents a new rule of evidence to burden plaintiffs in racial-gerrymandering cases. As of today, courts must draw an adverse inference against those plaintiffs when they do not submit a so-called alternative map—no matter how much proof of a constitutional violation they otherwise present." <small>(Dissenting Opinion by Associate Justice E. Kagan for Alexander, President of the South Carolina Senate v. South Carolina State Conference of the NAACP, 2024).</small>

"In cases without smoking-gun evidence, the only practical way to prove that a State considered race when drawing districts is to "show that the State's chosen map conflicts with traditional redistricting criteria. Judging a map's consistency or conflict with traditional districting principles requires a court to ascertain what kinds of maps should result from the application of those principles." <small>(Concurring Opinion by Associate Justice C. Thomas for Alexander, President of the South Carolina Senate v. South Carolina State Conference of the NAACP, 2024).</small>

"Indeed, as we have marked defined them, "traditional districting principles" are simply anything relevant to drawing districts other than race." <small>(Concurring Opinion by Associate Justice C. Thomas for Alexander, President of the South Carolina Senate v. South Carolina State Conference of the NAACP, 2024).</small>

There is clearly no new rule to the existing rule that was established in 1787. It is nothing more of the federal government undermining and wanting to take control of the electoral clauses.

It is the high court of the land trying to undermine these clauses and give more control to the legislative and executive branches to the General Government. The liberal movement within the federal government is to place more federalization control in state courts and up to the federal courts.

"Just seven years ago, this Court decided another racial-gerrymandering case, strikingly similar to this one. In *Cooper v. Harris*, the Court rejected the State's request for an alternative-map requirement; the dissent vehemently objected. (Alito, J., dissenting). The Court applied normal clear-error review, deferring to all plausible trial court findings. The dissent, invoking a presumption of good faith, instead deferred to all plausible arguments of the losing state defendant. (Dissenting Opinion by Associate Justice E. Kagan for Alexander, President of the South Carolina Senate v. South Carolina State Conference of the NAACP, 2024).

"Today, for all practical purposes, the *Cooper* dissent becomes law." (Dissenting Opinion by Associate Justice E. Kagan for Alexander, President of the South Carolina Senate v. South Carolina State Conference of the NAACP, 2024).

Actually, for practical reasons, the Cooper dissent becomes a precedent to the doctrine of state sovereignty.

The Cooper decision won the majority in 2017 because it established that the North Carolina state legislature relied too heavily on race in redrawing two congressional districts after the 2010 census.

"The Constitution does not offer "a theory for defining effective participation in representative government." (Concurring Opinion by Associate Justice C. Thomas for Alexander, President of the South Carolina Senate v. South Carolina State Conference of the NAACP, 2024).

I quite disagree with this statement from Justice Thomas. The Constitution does offer a practice to define an effective participation in representative government. It is called the Ninth Amendment along with the Tenth Amendment. This whole Constitution is a citizen participation document for a better union government for these sovereign states.

* * *

Justice Thomas makes a very disturbing, but comprehensible comparison with this case and the landmark case ruling back in 1954. Let us discuss and analyze his statement and see where I can pinpoint who is incorrect in this assessment. The media pundits or Justice Clarence Thomas.

"The view of equity required to justify a judicial map-drawing power emerged in the 1950s. The court's "impatience with the pace of desegregation" caused by resistance to *Brown v. Board of Education*, 347 U.S. 483 (1954), "led us to approve... extraordinary remedial measures," *Missouri v. Jenkins*, 515 U.S. 70, 125 (1995) (THOMAS, j., concurring). In the follow-up case to *Brown*, the Court considered "the manner in which relief [was] to be accorded" for vindication of "the fundamental principle that racial discrimination in public education is unconstitutional." *Brown v. Board of Education*, 349 U.S. 294, 298 (1955)." (Concurring Opinion by Associate Justice C. Thomas for Alexander, President of the South Carolina Senate v. South Carolina State Conference of the NAACP, 2024).

"That understanding may have justified temporary to "overcome the widespread resistance to the dictates of the Constitution" prevalent at that time, but, as a general matter, "[s]uch extravagant uses of judicial power are at odds with the history and tradition of the equity power and the Framers' design. Federal Courts have the power to grant only the equitable relief "traditionally accorded by Courts of equity," not the flexible power to invent whatever new remedies may seem useful at the time." (Concurring Opinion by Associate Justice C. Thomas for Alexander, President of the South Carolina Senate v. South Carolina State Conference of the NAACP, 2024).

The "extravagant judicial power" granted by the Federal Courts used in 1954 was quick and just. The Framers' constitutional judicial framework designed it to avert any abuse of power. Also, it brings forth a correct constitutional interpretation of all amendments and clauses. The remedy performed in the case of *Brown* and the follow-up cases of *Brown* were done appropriately. Even though, the original framers did not draft the Fourteenth Amendment. What Justice Thomas is trying to state here is that there is no use of extravagant of judicial power on a case regarding the electoral clauses. Regarding a case of segregation of inequality under law, the use of extravagant judicial power is rightly justified.

Liberal and unconstitutional media pundits are trying to alert the public that Justice Thomas is trying to not only undermine the Electoral Clauses but also undermine and bring forth a ruling to overturn *Brown v. Board of Education*. If he would plan to present a plan to overturn the desegregation of schools or end the course of interracial marriage. Then he would be overturning his own marriage and his family's own future.

* * *

"I continue to believe that "[t]he matters the Court has set out to resolve in vote dilution cases are... not questions of law," and that "they are not readily subjected to any judicially manageable standards. Racial

gerrymandering and vote dilution claims—at a mini-
mum, those challenging congressional districts—are
nonjusticiable for an additional reason: The Elections
Clause makes a "textually demonstrable constitutional
commitment to oversee congressional districting to
"a coordinate political department," Congress. And,
no other constitutional provision overcomes that commitment to Congress. The Constitution contemplates
no role for the federal courts in the districting pro-
cess." (Concurring Opinion by Associate Justice C. Thomas for Alexander,
President of the South Carolina Senate v. South Carolina State Conference of the
NAACP, 2024).

The Constitution contemplates no role for the federal courts in the districting process, or for any State's
electoral standards process.

It is a well-known constitutional fact, as we have
seen in other rulings, in where most of the high court
justices state the obvious in the role of the courts
regarding the electoral clauses. There is nothing in
our principled document to state the courts are here to
dictate electoral standards and procedures of the individual sovereign States. The only entity to not enforce
but administer the electoral standards of each state is
the national Congress.

"Although States have the initial duty to draw
district lines, the Elections Clause commits exclusive supervisory authority over the States' drawing
of congressional districts to Congress—not federal
courts. It provides: "The Times, Places, and Manner
of holding Elections for Senators and Representatives,
shall be prescribed in each State by the Legislature

thereof; but the Congress may at any time by Law or alter such Regulations, except as to the Places of chusing Senators," Art., I, Section IV, cl., I." (Concurring Opinion by Associate Justice C. Thomas for Alexander, President of the South Carolina Senate v. South Carolina State Conference of the NAACP, 2024).

This is where the problem arises in who should administer the States' electoral codes. It is within the Constitution that it is Congress, but the Courts wants to be the ones dictating this power. Then comes the executive branch of the General Government that wants to propose and enforce a national electoral directive.

Congress created the Fifteenth Amendment, guaranteeing all citizens' right to vote. From that guaranteed right to vote, Congress created the Voting Rights Act of 1965 protection to that right to vote. But that is as far as Congress can go for the voter's guaranteed for the right to vote.

The electoral clauses are quite clear, "The times, places and manner of holding elections for senators and representatives, shall be prescribed in each state legislature."

The "manner of holding elections" and "shall be prescribed in each state legislature," are two statements from the clause that there is no room for a different interpretation. This means that each state legislature has the power to dictate the electoral standards and procedures.

This is the problem that we are facing. Ever since state legislatures in the late nineteenth to mid-twentieth centuries were suppressing minority voters.

Everybody became skeptic of today's actions of many state legislatures.

If the voter's right to vote has not been compromised or denied, and voters follow the standards and procedures correctly. Then nothing should be called into a claim.

"In the electoral sphere especially, where "ugly patterns of pervasive racial discrimination" have so long governed, we should demand better—of ourselves, of our political representatives, and most of all of this Court." (Dissenting Opinion by Associate Justice E. Kagan for Alexander, President of the South Carolina Senate v. South Carolina State Conference of the NAACP, 2024).

"But, the Framers nowhere suggested the federal courts as a potential solution to those problems." (Concurring Opinion by Associate Justice C. Thomas for Alexander, President of the South Carolina Senate v. South Carolina State Conference of the NAACP, 2024).

The federal government, this high court, whether a conservative constitutional majority or a liberal constitutional majority, will always try to undermine the state's powers on the electoral clauses. The dream of some justices is to federalize the state courts but to the even extreme of federalizing our electoral system.

We saw it in 2000, 2020 and in the 2021 congressional session where federal advocates tried to undermine this clause. The Gore team in 2000 tried to undermine the Florida electoral standards to use Texas' standards. They even tried to convince the high court to undermine it at a federal level. Let us not go far as that, in 2020, the Trump team tried to undermine two states and even tried to bring forth a case to the high court, but it was denied. The high court dismissed the state of Texas tried to sue other states' electoral codes and indeed lacks Article III, *Texas v. Pennsylvania*, 2020. But, also applied Article III, but Article I, section IV, clause I and Article II, section I, clause II. Which those other clauses were applied in this dismissal. Then we saw the national Congress try to apply a federal act to make a national voting standard which was voted down.

These electoral clauses are still in the Constitution, and all citizens, and the federal government must respect its state sovereign doctrine despite political party or group affiliations.

We have seen them, not only to undermine the electoral clauses. But they have undermined commerce clause and even the naturalization clause. This latest court ruling is to continue to set forth a case for federalization of our state sovereign doctrine. They will not stop till the sovereign states will stand their ground to let the states govern themselves as the Constitution's sees fit with no abuse or control of power.

There is one thing true and justified by Justice Kagan. We should demand better representation of our state legislators to respect and trust our rights from the federal constitution and each state constitution. It is our state legislative representation that counts more than our federal congressional delegation. That is where the representation begins to protect our individual rights as well as our state sovereign doctrine rights. The courts are also here to protect our rights, but they must never be seen to overstep their boundaries. This is something that all high court justices and even the Chief Justice must always try to respect it.

There would be future federalization cases against the states' electoral clauses and rights. It must never come to light, and we must resist that unconstitutional temptation at all costs. The future of our long-lasting American republic of sovereign States depends on our fight to preserve its federalism value.

2024 Election (Insider Update)

Article I, Section IV, Clause I

"The Times, Places and Manner of holding Elections for Senators and Representatives, shall be prescribed in each State by the Legislature thereof; but the Congress may at any time by Law make or alter such Regulations, except as to the Places of chusing [sic] Senators.

Article II, Section I, Clause II

"Each State shall appoint, in such Manner as the Legislature thereof may direct, a Number of Electors, equal to the whole Number of Senators and Representatives to which the State may be entitled in the Congress: but no Senator or Representative, or Person holding an Office of Trust or Profit under the United States, shall be appointed an Elector.

On November 5, 2024, republican presidential candidate Donald J. Trump won a non-consecutive (second term) to the White House. It was a crazy electoral season, all due thanks to the new republican-progressive populist movement. A movement that started Donald Trump to gain populist momentum.

The MAGA republicans were not only the ones being unconstitutional during this campaign. Moderate republicans and democrats were also being unconstitutional. All sides were not respecting the rules of federalism and the electoral clauses of our federal Constitution.

Both sides played this populist shady game to gain a celebrity media status towards the populist masses. To gain sympathy for their unfortunate character short comings and lousy campaign platform proposals.

What can I say about the 2024 electoral campaign in four words? "Useless amateur theatrics show." I would say that every single election has had their useless, amateur theatrics show, but this one really takes the crowning achievement of uselessness.

The elections that I have pointed in this book has had their uselessness, but they also had a unconstitutional mind to it as it did this one and 2020 election. And to mention 2024, it was filled with unconstitutionally sentiment.

The fight in the Colorado state to get rid of Donald Trump from their ballot by using a federal government Fourteenth Amendment challenge was futile and unnecessary. For a state to use that sort of an amendment was completely laughable. But this just proves that the American people are ignorant to the complete language of the entire Constitution.

Sovereign states do not need a federally enumerated article to submit a challenge to remove a candidate from their ballot. States have had that power since before the civil war amendments were added and they still have that power as of today. Even the three most liberal supreme court jurists have stated the obvious. More obvious than the conservative majority supreme court jurists. And of course, yet again, after the high court ruled that Colorado cannot enforce their electoral clauses with a Fourteenth Amendment challenge. The media and the anti-Trump organizations failed to really implement appropriate legislation to ban Donald J. Trump from the ballot. As it is their duty to perform since it is in the federal Constitution.

Then of course, the federal criminal trials of Donald J. Trump in where this individual was founded guilty on thirty-four federal counts. Donald J. Trump is the first president-elect convicted federal criminal. Can a convicted criminal be sworn in as our chief executive of this union? That is a question to be defined not by the courts, but by Congress.

The high court in another court decision during this turbulent election season brought up to tell us the definition of the chief executive's official and unofficial acts.

In this court ruling of *Donald Trump v. United States*, 2024, the high court did not favor Trump or the liberal progressive establishment targeting the former president. The high court was stating the obvious, and yet we wasted taxpayer's dollars in something that we already knew but needed to be advised. But we needed to be advised because yet again, the American people are completely oblivious to the present situation and current language of the Constitution.

Left-wing individuals and media pundits when they read this ruling, they started screaming that they made Donald J. Trump into an elected despot king.

Right-wing individuals and media pundits when they read this ruling, they started celebrating that Trump won and he has full immunity on everything.

Nothing could be further from the truth if people would have read this ruling, written by Chief Justice John Roberts on presidential immunity:

"The President enjoys no immunity for his unofficial acts, and not everything the President does is official. The President is not above the law."

Of course, people forget to read and interpret it in their words filled with rage and emotions. Rather than reading these opinions with a constitutional open and common-sense mind. We would not be having these unfortunate and unnecessary outbursts.

The president for his official acts, as defined in the Constitution and later advised by the high court are protected with immunity. But for his unofficial acts, that occurred on January 6, 2021 are not protected with immunity and therefore the high court returned these questions back to the lower court for further review. This is not a win for Donald Trump or a loss for the Constitution.

This is a win for the American people to educate themselves plenty in the fine words of this principled document. To read for themselves, rather than to be told by somebody else, especially the high court of the land.

After this ruling came about, the election campaign continued to new amateur theatric shows. Of course, the MAGA crowd, the anti-Trump crowd, and media outlets fell into this campaign circus that was 2024.

Then came June 13, 2024, in Butler, Pennsylvania where an alleged assassin tried to assassinate Donald J. Trump. I cannot comment on this turn of events. All I can do is question all the actions that occurred on that day. Trump is a man of pure showmanship and I question this event, only because it is too obvious not to question all what happened on that day.

Theodore Roosevelt was the first president to also survive an assassin's bullet but carried on with his campaign speech. To my knowledge, T.R. did not make any photo-op to gain populist momentum.

After that event, the amateur theatrics did not slow down but did not show any rampant movement until the night of the first and only presidential debate. Prior to the debate, then-vice-presidential candidate J.D. Vance made an outrageous comment that "migrants from Haiti were eating the pets of residents of an obscure Ohio town." If that was a laughingstock moment for Trump and people instead of giving him media attention, should have blocked him. I believe that he would not have been elected the forty-seventh president.

Then after the embarrassing and bad performance of Trump at the debate. It appeared that there was another attempted assassination attempt on his life, but this time the assumed assassin was apprehended by Secret Service and local police. Again, I only question these actions that we as Americans must question to bring answers to our first amendment right.

So far, Donald J. Trump was campaigning heavily in the sovereign state of Pennsylvania and in certain states of what I like to call the Scandinavian-Midwest states, like Michigan.

As you read in the other chapters, I point out that in presidential elections, the vote that matters are the electoral vote. The popular vote is meaningless, as we have seen in previous elections. Especially the ones that I discuss in this book. As most of the framers have interpreted that the states built the Constitution. It is a Constitution made by the states. The States control their elections, the entire elections and it never cross any of the framers' mind that they were to establish a centralized electoral commission or committee.

Both the MAGA crowd and liberal-democrat crowd want somehow for the federal government to intervene, influence, and meddle in several state electoral procedures and standards. One thing listed in the electoral clauses is that the national government has no place to dictate electoral standards onto the states.

We have seen the republicans always seeking the courts to intervene, especially the high court, while the democrats are always seeking congressional electoral directives. Both forms are unconstitutional and goes against the state sovereign doctrine as listed in the electoral clauses. In 2020, we saw republicans seeking the high court to intervene via-Texas, for them to ask Pennsylvania and Wisconsin to set their standards in accordance with Texas' standards. Déjà vu because it was the same strategy, but the democrats were seeking that standard to be applied but in Florida. The only one that can change, amend, and set their own standards is the state legislature of their state. If the state legislature wishes to request for their state court to play an integral part in their electoral standards, then so be it. But so far, no state assembly has applied that directive.

In 2024, republicans asked the high court to intervene in an electoral standard plan in Pennsylvania.

The Supreme Court of Pennsylvania granted permission to proceed to be counted in a very unorthodox, but legal fashion.

"This case concerns a recent decision of the Supreme Court of Pennsylvania that adopted a controversial interpretation of important provisions of the Pennsylvania Election Code. Specifically, the court held that a provisional ballot must be counted even if the voter previously submitted an invalid mail-in-ballot within the time required by law." (Opinion on Application for Stay on Republican National Committee, et., al. v. Faith Genser, et., al. by Associate Justice Samuel Alito, 2024).

"The applicants contend that this interpretation flouts the plain meaning of the state election code, see Pa. Cons. Stat. Section 3050(a.4)(5)(ii)(2019), and that the interpretation is so far afield that it violates the Elections Clause and the Electors Clause of the Constitution of the United States. See Art. I, Section 4, cl. 1; Art II, Section 1, cl. 2; *Moore v. Harper*, 600 U.S. 1, 37 (2023)." (Opinion on Application for Stay on Republican National Committee, et., al. v. Faith Genser, et., al. by Associate Justice Samuel Alito, 2024).

The applicants and I share the same point of view. It is not the job of a state supreme court to rewrite an electoral law standard *unless* it is indicated by the state legislature.

This decision should have given the win to Vice-President Kamala Harris and running mate Tim Walz. Yet somehow it backfired to the populist extreme of MAGA masses that gave Pennsylvania the win to Donald Trump and JD Vance. This type of court decision is what I like to call poetic political justice.

"The application of the State Supreme Court's interpretation in the upcoming election is a matter of considerable importance, but even if we agreed with the applicant's federal constitutional argument (a question on which I express no view at this time), we could not prevent the consequences they fear." (Opinion on Application for Stay on Republican National Committee, et., al. v. Faith Genser, et., al. by Associate Justice Samuel Alito, 2024).

It is a question that no member of the general government of the United States; the executive branch, the national Congress, or the high court should have at any given point in time. These sorts of questions are for the state legislatures of all states, not for the state courts.

"And because the only state election officials who are parties in this case are the members of the board of elections in one small county, we cannot order other election boards to sequester affected ballots. For these reasons, I agree with the order denying the application." (Opinion on Application for Stay on Republican National Committee, et., al. v. Faith Genser, et., al. by Associate Justice Samuel Alito, 2024).

Did we learn a valuable lesson from this intrusion of the courts, federal and state in obstructing a clause that is clearly not in their purview of electoral enforcement? From their decision of Moore v. Harper, 2023, and now this stay denial to a state court's decision on a legislative electoral law standard. People need to stop seeking for federal government aid and help, plain and simple. As Associate Justice Clarence Thomas once stated, "But "federal courts cannot give answers simply because someone asks." Individuals need to have faith in their state powers, not in federal powers, and because of this, the federal executive branch will soon be in control by once again Donald J. Trump.

We cannot rely on the courts, federal. We must rely on the Constitution which gives the power of the states.

The state assembly of Pennsylvania was split in political party control. The republicans controlled the state house, while the democrats controlled the state senate. I have always said that "Whoever controls the state assembly, controls the states' electoral votes.

I can honestly say that this election of 2024 was brought upon dirty populism. This union of sovereign states has lost the will of the constitutional framers. We are no longer relying on our principled founding fathers on the Constitution. We are now relying on a new populist voting front, called Trumpism. Our electoral clauses granted power to the states are quickly soon will disappear to set a new standard, a full national popular voting standard.

I will focus on four states' electoral 2024 votes because they go against the federalism values our framers visioned.

Pennsylvania 22-24 session	State Assembly	DEM – 102 members	GOP– 100 members	2 seat difference
	State Senate	GOP – 28 members	DEM– 20 members	8 seat difference
Michigan 22-24 session	State Assembly	DEM – 56 members	GOP – 54 members	2 seat difference
	State Senate	DEM – 20 members	GOP – 18 members	2 seat difference
Nevada 22-24 session	State Assembly	DEM – 28 members	GOP – 14 members	14 seat difference
	State Senate	DEM – 13 members	GOP – 8 members	5 seat difference
North Carolina 22-24 session	State Assembly	GOP – 71 members	DEM – 49 members	22 seat difference
	State Senate	GOP – 30 members	DEM – 20 members	10 seat difference

The make-up of these state legislatures is too tight to see who holds most electoral votes. Therefore, these become battleground states because of the petty two-party system, this union has become today.

Despite a clear difference between the legislative made-up and popular made-up of census statistics, in this republic of sovereign states, the legislature holds the power.

Florida 22-24 session	State Assembly	GOP – 85 members	DEM – 35 members	50 seat difference
	State Senate	GOP – 28 members	DEM – 12 members	16 seat difference
California 23-24 session	State Assembly	DEM – 62 members	GOP – 17 members	45 seat difference
	State Senate	DEM – 31 members	GOP – 9 members	22 seat difference

The make-up of these state legislatures is way best described to be a clear winning of their electoral votes with no clear sense to call a fraud or stop a steal. Why come Donald Trump or Kamala Harris does not call for an investigation for a vote count? The reason behind it is because it is a fight, they know they will lose.

Again, I still believe that whatever political party or movement controls that state legislature, controls these votes. Even with such razor thin seat differences, the electoral vote must go with who controls the slate of electors…hence who controls the state legislature.

But we are moving closer and closer to a populist democracy and away from our republic ideals that our framers entrusted us to follow in our Constitution. I surely hope that we return to these principled republic ideals and never to these progressive democratic populist ideals that are a ruin to this beautiful American republic.

Bibliography

CHAPTER I

The One-Party Presidential Contest: Adams, Jackson, and the 1824's Five-Horse Race, Donald Ratcliffe, University of Press Kansas, 2015

Against the Force Bill, by John C. Calhoun, 15 & 16 February 1833

Michael R. Pence, former vice president of the United States, March 15, 2024

Donald Trump on The Hill article by Brett Samuels, 09/17/23

CHAPTER II

By One Vote: The Disputed Presidential Election of 1876, Michael F. Holt, University of Press Kansas, 2008

Trump asked Ted Cruz to argue Texas election lawsuit if it reaches Supreme Court, by Betsy Klein, Jim Acosta, and Caroline Kennedy, CNN, Wed., December 09, 2020

CHAPTER III

Per Curiam Opinion of the United States Supreme Court on Bush v. Gore, 2000

Bibliography

Concurring Opinion on Bush v. Gore by Chief Justice
William Rehnquist, 2000

Dissenting Opinion on Bush v. Gore by Associate Justice
John Paul Stevens, 2000

Dissenting Opinion on Bush v. Gore by Associate Justice
Ruth Bader Ginsburg, 2000

CHAPTER IV

Norma Anderson, et. al., v. Jena Griswold, Per Curiam
decision on December 19, 2023

Full List of States Wanting to Kick Trump off Ballot and
Where Cases Stand, Newsweek, Andrew Stanton,
weekend staff writer, December 21, 2023

Donald J. Trump v. Norma Anderson, 2024, Oral
Argument of Jonathan F. Mitchell, Petitioner

Oral Arguments of Donald J. Trump v. Norma Anderson,
2024, Associate Justice Sonia Sotomayor

Oral Arguments of Donald J. Trump v. Norma Anderson,
2024, Associate Justice Samuel Alito

Oral Arguments of Donald J. Trump v. Norma Anderson,
2024, Associate Justice Brett Kavanaugh

Oral Arguments of Donald J. Trump v. Norma Anderson,
2024, Associate Justice Elena Kagan

Oral Arguments of Donald J. Trump v. Norma Anderson,
2024, Associate Justice Amy Comey Barrett

Oral Arguments of Donald J. Trump v. Norma Anderson,
2024, Associate Justice Neil Gorsuch

Oral Arguments of Donald J. Trump v. Norma Anderson,
2024, Associate Justice Ketanji Jackson

CHAPTER V

Bibliography

Dissenting Opinion on Chisom v. Roemer, Governor of Louisiana, Et Al. by Associate Justice Antonin Scalia, 1990

Opinion Brief on Chisom v. Roemer, Governor of Louisiana, Et Al. by Associate Justice John Paul Stevens, 1990

Report of the Comm'n on Fed. Election Reform, Building Confidence in U.S. Elections 46 (Sept. 2005)

Oral Argument of Mr. David H. Thompson, on behalf of the petitioners on Moore v. Harper, December 7, 2022

Oral Question of Chief Justice John Roberts on Moore v. Harper, December 7, 2022

Oral Question of Associate Justice Sonia Sotomayor on Moore v. Harper, December 7, 2022

Oral Question of Associate Justice Kentanji Brown Jackson on Moore v. Harper, December 7, 2022

Oral Question of Associate Justice Samuel Alito on Moore v. Harper, December 7, 2022

Oral Question of Associate Justice Brett Kavanaugh on Moore v. Harper, December 7, 2022

Oral Argument of Mr. Neal K. Katyal, on behalf of the respondents on Moore v. Harper, December 7, 2022

Oral Question of Associate Justice Neil Gorsuch on Moore v. Harper, December 7, 2022

Judgment syllabus of Moore v. Harper, 2023

Opinion of the Court for Moore v. Harper, 2023 by Chief Justice John Roberts

Concurring Opinion of the Court for Moore v. Harper, 2023 by Associate Justice Brett Kavanaugh

Dissenting Opinion of the Court for Moore v. Harper, 2023 by Associate Justice Clarence Thomas

CHAPTER IV

LISTEN ON SPREAKER, SPOTIFY,
I ♥ RADIO, GOOGLE PODCASTS

STATES RIGHTS RADIO

E-Mail: statesrightsradio@mail.com
Instagram: state.rights.radio